Penguin English
Introducing Language Awareness

Leo van Lier is Professor of Educational Linguistics at the Monterey Institute of International Studies in California. He grew up in the Netherlands, did his graduate studies in England (he holds a Ph.D. in Linguistics from the University of Lancaster), and has worked in many countries, including the Netherlands, England, Denmark and Mexico. He also worked on a bilingual education project in Puno, Peru, for two years. He has taught graduate courses in educational linguistics and trained teachers in the US since 1984. He is very interested in the development of effective and innovative language pedagogies, including bilingual education, and has written several books and numerous articles on the subject.

Ronald Carter is Professor of Modern English Language in the Department of English Studies at the University of Nottingham. He is the author of many books on applied linguistics and was the National Co-ordinator for the LINC (Language in the National Curriculum) project from 1989 to 1992.

David Nunan is Professor of Applied Linguistics and Director of the English Centre at the University of Hong Kong. He has worked as a TESOL teacher, teacher educator, curriculum designer, and materials writer and consultant in Britain and overseas and is the author of many books on applied linguistics and ELT.

Other Titles in the Series

Introducing

LANGUAGE

AWARENESS

Leo van Lier

Series Editors:
Ronald Carter and David Nunan

PENGUIN
ENGLISH

PENGUIN ENGLISH

Published by the Penguin Group
Penguin Books Ltd, 27 Wrights Lane, London W8 5TZ, England
Penguin Books USA Inc., 375 Hudson Street, New York, New York 10014, USA
Penguin Books Australia Ltd, Ringwood, Victoria, Australia
Penguin Books Canada Ltd, 10 Alcorn Avenue, Toronto, Ontario, Canada M4V 3B2
Penguin Books (NZ) Ltd, 182–190 Wairau Road, Auckland 10, New Zealand

Penguin Books Ltd, Registered Offices: Harmondsworth, Middlesex, England

First published 1995
1 3 5 7 9 10 8 6 4 2

The moral right of the author has been asserted

Typeset by Datix International Limited, Bungay, Suffolk
Printed in England by Clays Ltd, St Ives plc
Filmset in 10/13 pt Monophoto Times

It is well we should become aware of what we are doing when we speak, of the ancient, fragile, and (well used) immensely potent instruments that words are.

C. S. Lewis *Studies in Words*

Water is round in a round receptacle and square in a square one, but water itself has no particular shape. People often forget that.

The teaching of Buddha

The insights provided by work in applied linguistics can be of genuine support to all teachers facing the many complex demands of language learning and teaching. The Penguin English *Introducing Applied Linguistics* series aims to provide short, clear and accessible guides to key topics – helping teachers to keep abreast of this rapidly developing field by explaining recent research and its relevance to common problems and concerns. The books are designed for practical use: they focus on recognizable classroom contexts, suggest problem-solving approaches, and include activities and questions for further study.

Introducing Applied Linguistics presumes an increasing convergence of interest among all English language teachers, and it aims to be relevant both to teachers of English as a second or foreign language and to teachers of English as a mother tongue. As the relationship between linguistics and language teaching continues to develop, so the need grows for books which introduce the field. This series has been developed to meet that need.

The words that appear in **bold** type are
explained in the glossary.

Acknowledgements

Many of the ideas in this book started in linguistics courses for language teachers. I want to thank several generations of graduate students at the Monterey Institute of International Studies for helping me develop my views on language awareness. Kim Marie Cole made many critical and imaginative contributions over several years of collaboration, including a teamtaught course on Language Analysis in 1992. Other colleagues and friends have also given encouragement and valuable advice, among them Larry and Judith Grimes, whose hospitable Missouri farm is an ideal (and relaxed) context for discussions of language awareness, Betty Lou Leaver, President of the American Global Studies Institute, Roxy Harris of Thames Valley University, and Josep Cots of the University of Lleida. Thanks also to fellow members of the Association for Language Awareness and, as always, to Aida, Jan and Marcus for their support.

The publishers make grateful acknowledgement to the following for permission to reproduce copyright material: 'Chancellor Aims to Purge "What-Cha's and Aint's"' by Neil A. Lewis, copyright © 1995 by The New York Times Company, reprinted by permission; 'Teacher Should Reassess Project That Backfired' by Larry Meeks, reproduced by permission of Larry Meeks and Creators Syndicate.

Every effort has been made to trace copyright holders in every case. The publishers would be interested to hear from any not acknowledged here.

Contents

Introduction

Language is as important to human beings as water is to fish. Yet, it often seems that we go through life as unaware of language as we suppose the average fish is of the water it swims in. We just use language, without having a clear idea of how our lives and relationships are shaped by and through it. If it is poisoned, we may feel sick without knowing that it is poisoned language which makes us feel sick; if we are pushed in a certain direction without wanting to be, we may not know that language is pushing us in that direction.

This book is an awareness-raising exercise about language. The aim is to help the reader understand how language is used as a tool, how it relates to life's central activities, from learning to thinking to social relationships.

Language awareness can be defined as an understanding of the human faculty of language and its role in thinking, learning and social life. It includes an awareness of power and control through language, and of the intricate relationships between language and **culture**.

When we 'study language', we usually think of vocabulary lists, **grammar** exercises and proper pronunciation, spelling and punctuation. If we think a little further, we may include literary appreciation, academic reading and writing skills, or theoretical **linguistics**. None of these things are part of language awareness as envisaged in this book, nor is language awareness designed to replace any of them. Instead, we are trying to promote a new look at language, one that looks at language as a living thing rather than a dissected corpse. Instead of picking it apart and poking around at the bits and pieces (although we do a bit of that in chapter 2), we try to follow it around to see what it does. But since we are all language users, we will also reflect on what we do when we use language (so that language awareness will not be just a spectator sport).

Throughout the book there are awareness-raising activities which, I hope, are interesting and stimulating in their own right, but at the same time they are aimed at making the reader curious to find out more about one aspect of language or another, and lead to further study and investigation, perhaps using ideas mentioned in the Project section, or the suggestions for further reading at the end of the book. Very often the activities do not have one single or straightforward answer, but wherever I feel I can give useful comments or suggestions, these are provided either in the text or in the Key at the end of the book.

Language awareness is its own reward. Since language makes us into whatever we are, language awareness enriches all our experiences and gives us a sense of being more in control of our destiny, and to perceive the things that go on around us with greater clarity. At the same time this little book cannot give answers to all the questions that arise when we become aware of language. If the reader starts the book with a few questions, and ends up with a great many more, then I feel the book has served its purpose.

1 Language awareness: what, when and why?

This is the age of communication, of information super-highways, of networking and electronic mail. Job interviews stress teamwork and information-sharing over and above technical know-how, and politicians do some of their most important work on the daily TV talk shows. Talk, which was once primarily a family affair, to be conducted around the kitchen table, or perhaps with friends around the stove or at the coffee shop, is in the centre of the public stage and is now everywhere, stitched into the fabric of society with the needle and thread of technology, providing immediate feedback, information, and entertainment (or even 'infotainment') from everywhere to everyone, through a multiplicity of sources and media.

It is often said that the main thing distinguishing humans from other animals is language. Of course, many animals also communicate in quite efficient ways, as the dance of bees, the sounds of dolphins, and the concerted actions of armies of ants demonstrate. But we humans feel that language is at the very core of our existence, that it defines us and shapes our being more than any other asset we possess (actually, the ant, if we had a way of listening to it, might tell us the same thing). Language builds and cements our social relationships, helps us to think and allows us to reflect, is used first to educate us and subsequently by us to educate others. Without it no war can be declared nor peace announced, and neither ships nor babies can be named. Clearly, language is a vital area of study for a better understanding of ourselves and the improvement of our situation.

Yet, for all its importance, language as a field of scientific study, linguistics, is one of the most obscure and least understood of all academic pursuits. Psychologists, chemists, even astrophysicists, have no trouble answering the question, 'What do you do for a living?' Linguists, however, dread the question, since the answer 'I am a linguist' will inevitably be countered by 'How many languages do you speak?' or 'Which language do you teach?' Most people simply do not know what linguistics is or what a linguist does. The public, it sometimes appears, finds it easier to understand why someone should study the breathing of brine shrimp than derivational **morphology**.

At this point the reader may want to reflect on the subject of language and linguistics. What do you think of when you hear the term linguistics? What sorts of things or topics would you expect to find in a book on linguistics? And what definitely interests you about language, and what definitely does not?

1.1 When are we aware of language?

When we use language we are normally hardly aware of the physical, or formal, aspects of it. Language is like the air we breathe. We cannot do without it, but we do not often consciously pay attention to it. It is as if we look through language directly to the meanings that it conveys, and the thoughts that it expresses. This quality is often called the transparency of language. Michael Polanyi, in his classic book *Personal Knowledge* (1958), gives a nice example of this:

My correspondence arrives at my breakfast table in various languages, but my son understands only English. Having just finished reading a letter I may wish to pass it on to him, but I must check myself and look again to see in what language it was written. I am vividly aware of the meaning conveyed by the letter, yet know nothing whatever of its words. I have attended to them closely but only for what they mean and not for what they are as objects. If my understanding of the text were halting, or its expressions or its spelling were faulty, its words would arrest my attention. They would become slightly opaque and prevent my thought from passing through them unhindered to the things they signify. (page 57).

Two things are of special interest in the anecdote Polanyi tells us. The first one is when he says that he attended closely to the **words**, but only for their meaning, not for their form. The second point of interest is when he says that the words would 'arrest his attention' if he had a problem of understanding, or if the text were in some way faulty. There seem to be two different kinds of attention involved here, one which allows meanings to flow right through the words, another which blocks those meanings (or holds them back) while the words, the 'tools of thought' as it were, are scrutinized for some reason. When we talk of Language Awareness these two kinds of attention-paying must be sharply distinguished. Polanyi calls them subsidiary awareness (another term sometimes used is peripheral attention) and focal awareness, and considers them mutually exclusive (ibid, page 56).

This distinction is by no means peculiar to language use. The cyclist Polanyi describes below does the same thing. He rides straight ahead, focusing on the horizon or admiring the scenery, perhaps watching out for pedestrians and other cyclists at the same time. His balancing actions, meanwhile, are regulated by subsidiary awareness, unless he is an inexperienced cyclist, or the path is very irregular, or the front wheel is loose and wobbly, or his daughter sitting on the seat behind leans left or right to peer out at sights.

I have come to the conclusion that the principle by which the cyclist maintains his balance is not generally known. The rule observed by the cyclist is this. When he starts falling to the right he turns the handlebars to the right, so that the course of his bicycle is deflected along a curve towards the right. This results in a centrifugal force pushing the cyclist to the left and offsets the gravitational force dragging him down to the right. This manoeuvre presently throws the cyclist out of balance to the left, which he counteracts by turning the handlebars to the left; and so he continues to keep himself in balance by winding along a series of appropriate curvatures. A simple analysis shows that for a given angle of unbalance the curvature of each winding is inversely proportional to the square of the speed at which the cyclist is proceeding. (ibid., pages 49–50).

To take another example, we may be driving in our car and suddenly find we are in Centreville, without having any recollection of how we got there. Meanwhile, we have (we hope so, at least!) attended to all the traffic signs, overtaken other cars, stopped for pedestrians, and so on. Our subsidiary awareness was on the traffic, changing gear, the accelerator and so on, while our focal awareness was on the music playing on our new CD, or on the presentation we have to give at Centreville College.

Language awareness, as an educational goal, holds that it is necessary (or at least useful) at times to focus systematically on language in the second sense, of focal awareness. The two main reasons for this, and we will return to them in the next section, are:
— to deal with problems that occur in the language-using process;
— to reach higher levels of understanding and use.

1.2 Why language awareness?

Normally, our subsidiary awareness serves us quite well in everyday language use: it allows us to get on with life, work and the business of making sense of our world. However, at times, and for certain purposes, we need a higher level of awareness, a focal awareness, to accomplish some language-related or language-mediated goal. Here are some examples, adapted from everyday occurrences. I also invite you to think of some other instances, in yours or someone else's life, when language knowledge was important.

1a
Beth hears a political speech by a popular politician and finds that all her colleagues at work are quite impressed by it. Yet she has a feeling that the politician's words, fantastic though they sound, hide a

number of serious inconsistencies and insincerities. If she can take the politician's words (transcribed in today's newspaper) and is able to scrutinize them, she may be able to pinpoint exactly what it is that seems insincere in the speech, and discuss this with her colleagues. If she cannot, a vague 'feeling' of misgiving is insufficient to convince her colleagues, and possibly herself, that the speech should not be taken at face value.

1b

Ramon got in trouble at school for 'talking back' at a teacher. This is the second time in one week, and he is suspended for three days. He doesn't quite know what is wrong, and his parents don't either, since the exhortation to 'be polite' does not seem to be sufficient advice. What is really the matter here is that Ramon has not learned that you speak to kids in one way and to adults in another, in other words, he is not able to vary his **register**. *He talks to everybody in exactly the same way (the way he talks to the other kids), and adults find this insulting and disrespectful. Someone needs to guide Ramon to make him aware of the different ways of talking in his environment, encourage him to listen, and adapt his own speech according to the situation, so that he does not unintentionally upset his teachers and continually get into trouble.*

1c

Carla is a young Mexican woman studying English. She is going around London with a group of fellow-learners from different European countries, seeing the sights. She keeps calling everything she sees – Trafalgar Square, Westminster Abbey, Marble Arch, and so on – 'stupend', which is her 'Anglification' of the Spanish word 'estupendo'. Unfortunately, the way she says 'stupend' sounds very much like 'stupid', so her companions get the impression that she is very negative and stuck up about everything. She is in danger of getting a bad reputation and not making any friends. Someone – if not she herself – needs to realize that 'stupend' *is an adaptation of*

'estupendo', with the first and last vowels chopped off. Since this tactic works quite well for words like 'estupido' and 'esplendido', it is quite understandable that she would overgeneralize the vowel-chopping rule. Let's hope that someone points out the mistake to her in a gentle way, or that she becomes aware of it herself, before people start disliking and avoiding her!
(Author's data)

These examples suggest that there may be important reasons for bringing aspects of language into focal awareness, in order to solve problems, reach higher levels of skill in some particular area, or to think more critically and independently about important issues.

One can find a number of other reasons for raising language awareness, for example if one's job or profession requires frequent, efficient, or precise language use, such as in teaching, the legal professions, sales and marketing, psychotherapy and journalism. Further, given the close relationships between language and culture, cross-cultural communication, both within one's own multicultural and multi-ethnic environment and in international contacts, requires a much higher level of linguistic awareness than a monolingual, homogeneous existence does.

Finally, we tend to have quite strong and deep-seated opinions about language-related issues, though very often these opinions are unconscious or tacit, rather than overt, and many times they might bear bringing into the open for close scrutiny and possible amendment.

In order to encourage you to examine some of your opinions about language I offer the following diagnostic quiz. A warning is in order: the answer may not be a straightforward true or false, but perhaps more of an 'it depends', in which case it is instructive to examine what sorts of things a reasonable answer might depend on. Some feedback (on this and other tasks) is given in the Key to activities section at the end of the book.

ACTIVITY

1d

Test your knowledge of language

Mark the following statements true (T) or false (F). Asterisk (*) the ones you find most difficult to mark either T or F.

1. *Every native speaker of a language knows what is correct and what is incorrect in that language.*
2. *A **dialect** is a language without a written form.*
3. *The more you are exposed to a language, the faster you will learn it.*
4. *A language which does not change is a dead language.*
5. *Dialects are substandard deviations from a standard language.*
6. *A language is weakened when it borrows large numbers of words from other languages.*
7. *Some languages sound more beautiful than other languages.*
8. *Some words are 'dirty', some are 'clean', by their very nature.*
9. *Regardless of how many people use <u>ain't</u>, it is still not correct in English.*
10. *The rules of a language can be explained because they are logical.*

(Author's data)

1.3 Language awareness in education

There was a time, from the ancient Greeks to the late Middle Ages, when language was central in educational practices, in the form of the three branches of the *trivium*: grammar, logic, and rhetoric. Then, increasingly, language study became separated from other subjects such as maths and science, and became merely one other subject (or several, in places where foreign languages were taught). As a result, language lost its centrality and relevance as an

7

educational focal point, and it became difficult to see how it connected to other parts of the curriculum. Grammar was taught as a set of mechanical skills, as a series of intellectual puzzles, or as a code of 'proper' linguistic behaviour, that is, as prescriptive grammar, which lays down laws as to how we ought to speak, spell, compose and so on. In the educational process, language was alienated from most of its natural uses, and many readers may have unpleasant memories of naming parts of speech, drawing various diagrams and trees, and endless lists of spelling words. Unsurprisingly, this kind of language work was (and is!) not very popular with most students.

The next step, if it occurred at all (it did so in many schools in Great Britain and the US, but perhaps not so much in some other countries), was to neglect language teaching entirely, limiting instruction to basic literacy skills, followed by the study of literature. It seemed as if language itself (that is, apart from literature), could only be taught badly, so that it was preferable not to teach it at all.

The consequences of this separation or neglect of language education are hard to pinpoint, especially if one wants to move beyond prescriptive, imprecise and rather superficial complaints of the kind that students do not know how to spell correctly or speak properly. However, there has been a steadily increasing body of opinion claiming serious and far-reaching consequences for the present-day neglect of systematic language education, coupled with a variety of suggestions on what to do about it.

There is a perennial debate in many parts of the world between those who emphasize such things as correct spelling, rules of grammar, vocabulary use and proper pronunciation (linguistic etiquette, we might say), and those who take a more *laissez-faire* view of correctness, and consider that what is said is more important than how it is said. For example, in the US proponents of phonics (an approach to reading and writing instruction which uses a careful introduction of sounds and letters) and whole language (which stresses free expression, meaningful language use, and rich language experience) are always on opposite corners in the debate about how to teach reading and writing. The former accuse the latter of producing bad spellers and careless readers and writers, and in return are accused of dulling children's creativity and motivation by using artificial and boring texts of the '*See Spot run*' variety.

In Britain, particularly with the new National Curriculum, there is strong disagreement between those who see Knowledge About Language (KAL) as basically a return to traditional values of correct usage (grammar, spelling etc) and those who take a more **critical** and meaning-oriented approach which stresses the role of language in the sociocultural and political affairs of the people.

Such debates, which probably go on in one way or another in most countries in the world, have clearly been with us for a long time, and it does not look as if they are going to be resolved in the near future. Equally if not more acrimonious battles are fought over other language issues, such as bilingual education and the maintenance of immigrants' native languages, the intrusion into a language of large numbers of foreign loan words (such as English words into French, Japanese or many other languages), and the problems of teaching and learning foreign languages which seem to affect some countries far more than others (for example, the case of the Netherlands and Denmark is often compared to that of Great Britain, and the US, or France – you might like to reflect on your own explanations for such national differences in foreign-language learning success).

In chapter 6 we will examine several issues relating to language awareness and education in a little more detail. Meanwhile, the next few chapters will take a look at language itself, so that we can become aware of the complex nature of the phenomenon we are dealing with.

PROJECT

Language-awareness work relies on <u>noticing</u> the language around us and <u>examining</u> it in a critical manner. The best way to do this is by keeping a language log book, journal or diary, in which you note down pieces of language that, for one reason or another, capture your interest. Language awareness is an ongoing process of critical examination, and a way of looking at language.

You can learn to recognize and analyse the persuasive techniques of advertising, media and political language, conversations between men and women, people of different ages, backgrounds and cultures and so on. If you are a student you can readily find small research projects to do using the language around us, and if you are a teacher you can find – and encourage students to find – an abundance of authentic language to use in class.

SUMMARY

- Language is central to what it is to be human.
- Usually we are aware of language only in a subsidiary sense, but we bring it into focal awareness when there are problems, or when we need to reach higher levels of knowledge or skill.
- Language awareness can be of great importance in many aspects of life, including political, educational and social **contexts**.
- Language awareness opens up new possibilities for language education in schools, and avoids the extremes of prescribed correctness and utter neglect.

2 Building blocks of language

Every time my car breaks down I have to take it to a garage to be fixed, and in most cases pay a fairly hefty bill. Every time that happens, my neighbour across the street comes over to ask what was wrong and how much I paid, letting me know in no uncertain terms how much I was ripped off, and how much I could have saved if I had been smart enough to fix the problem myself (he, of course, does all his own repairs).

When something goes wrong with our language use, perhaps because we do not have the words to express what we want to, or we have problems interpreting an important message, there is no 'language garage' we can go to. Talking to family and friends can help a great deal, but in the last analysis we have to repair our own language problems. In order to be able to do this, some knowledge of the parts and the tools of which language consists is necessary. This chapter will look at these basic elements of language, without however going into a full linguistic analysis.

The experiences in our life, whether social or physical, are not neatly structured into clear-cut patterns and systems. Rather, we tend to create our own ways of dealing with things as we go along, often muddling through, relying on 'the ways things are done around here' (a simple, yet effective definition of culture I came across at a workshop). In their influential book, *The Social Construction of Reality*, Berger and Luckmann (1966) call much of our superficial knowledge, which is just sufficient to get by, recipe knowledge. This is the kind of knowledge we have of many complicated structures in our life, including cars, telephones and VCRs, but also the tax system, insurance, banking, education, the adolescent mind, friendship, prejudice and numerous other issues which confront us every day. We know, or hope, that we can navigate our way through the enormous complexity of our world, and we trust, when something is over our head, that we can find someone to help us out, whether it is a mechanic, an accountant, an insurance broker, a teacher, a neighbour, or a friend.

2.1 The basic nuts and bolts

Language is also one of the complex structures in our world, indeed, one of the most complex ones, and by and large we only have recipe knowledge of it. We know how to use it, but we may find it very difficult at times to use it effectively. Above, I mentioned that language is usually transparent, that meanings seem just to go right through it. It is like a window which we only notice when it gets dirty. However, unlike a window which may be kept spotlessly clean just with a rag and some cleaning liquid, language seems to have inherent blemishes and weak spots which we continually have to work to overcome and patch up. Language is never quite transparent, but that does not mean that it is easy for us to use it as we wish.

Many people realize the problematic nature of language, and the huge popularity of books such as Deborah Tannen's *That's Not What I Meant* (1987), and *You Just Don't Understand* (1990), show that we are keen to understand language better, and to use it to solve some of our problems (which, indeed, may be language problems, especially in such areas as personal and professional relationships).

Understanding language better, being aware of what it is and what it does, what we and other people do through and with it, is therefore of the utmost importance if we want to improve our lives. This is one area in which recipe knowledge will not suffice, in fact, in which it can be quite dangerous.

In this chapter I will survey the 'nuts and bolts' of language, the way in which it is put together. This may seem some way removed from critical thinking and consciousness, but as I said above it is essential to know the materials and the tools we have at our disposal to be critical and conscious with. Just like the carpenter needs to be familiar with the nature and characteristics of various kinds of wood, and needs to know what the purpose is of all the things in the tool box, as well as what to do with them, we need to become aware of the texture, the structure and the function of the different parts of language.

ACTIVITY

To begin with, I invite you to list here all the units or 'pieces' of language you can think of, from the very smallest to the largest (including word, sentence and so on):

(smallest)

(biggest)

Next, study the concepts in the box below, and check how many of these occur in your list in the box above. Are there any concepts in your list that do not occur in the box below? Do they include such words as **syllable**, **utterance**, *paragraph*, *story*? If so, you have come up with an excellent example of why any single classification, any one hierarchy of units, will never suffice to capture the complexity of language (for one thing, the list may be different if you are thinking of spoken or of written language). These are points we will come back to later.

2a

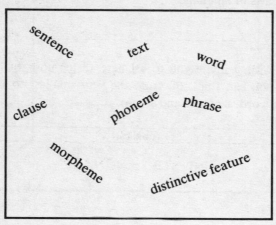

(Author's data)

Let us now arrange the units in the box above in order of size, primarily to illustrate the various traditional fields of study in linguistics, and as a starting point for more in-depth discussion.

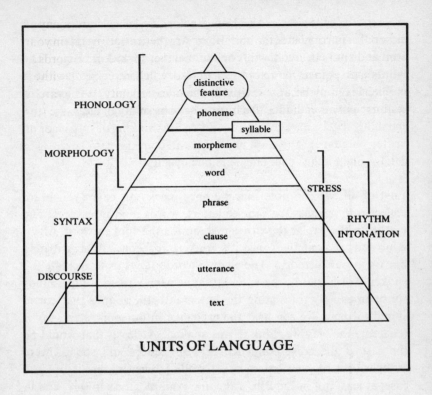

UNITS OF LANGUAGE

To illustrate this traditional approach to language in terms of the bits and pieces by means of which it is put together, let us examine a small strip of language from an everyday event: a family breakfast.

2b

A: Can I have some more milk, please?
B: Sure, just a second.
(Author's data)

This is one of the hundreds of little exchanges that occur between people every day. The language use here is entirely transparent, in the sense introduced in the last chapter, since we hardly expect either the participants (A and B) or any potential overhearers to stop and study the words in terms of their forms and meanings. The words are spoken, the relevant actions are accomplished, and that is that. Precisely because the exchange is so ordinary, it is useful to examine how it embodies the inner workings of language.

2.1.1   Sight and sound: language and opacity

First of all, we can note that we have marks on paper which are collected in groups. We can see letters, words, and utterances. The marks on the paper, the writing, stand for the spoken word, which is no longer available (once it's spoken, it's gone, though it may live on in our memory). The written word allows us to recreate the spoken word, that is, the letters (graphemes) correspond to sounds (**phonemes**). By translating the letters into the sounds that correspond to them, we can hear the exchange in our mind's ear, say it (enact it) the way we think it was spoken. At least, that would be the case if the correspondence between letters and sounds were straightforward: one letter, one sound. However, this is not the case, at least not in English. Take, for example, the s in *sure*, and in *second*, or the o in *more*, and in *second*. To complicate matters further, some letters may not correspond to any sound: the o in *some*, for example, was not pronounced at all: *some more* was pronounced as *smore*.

I do not want to go into the complexities of reading, or of learning to read, here, but it is important to realize that letter and sound are two different concepts and that, as a consequence, written and spoken language can be quite different. The less directly the written word reflects the spoken one, the more opaque we might call the relationship. Languages differ in terms of the degree of opacity there is between their written and spoken representations. Here is an informal ordering of some European languages:

2c

more opaque				less opaque
English	Danish	French	Spanish	Finnish
|	|	|	|	|
thought	morgon	deux	dedo	kukka
|	|	|	|	|
θɔːt	mɔːn	dø	deðo	kukːa

(Author's data)

Languages that are relatively opaque, such as English, need a **phonetic alphabet** of some kind in order to represent the sounds in the language accurately, both for the purposes of linguistic study and comparison, and for foreign students. Just think of the many ways in which the *ough* combination can be pronounced (in words like, *ought, plough, tough* and so on). It would facilitate the study of phonetics and pronunciation greatly if there were one list of symbols, a <u>phonetic alphabet</u>, which could be used to reproduce all speech sounds accurately, regardless of which language they were used in. For example, one might read

ˈʃtaxəl, ʃvəm

and be able to pronounce it exactly the way a German would, something that would be more difficult to accomplish, at least for speakers of English, with the word *Stachelschwein* (German for porcupine).

Over the years, various phonetic alphabets have been developed, the most well-known of them being the International Phonetic Alphabet, or IPA, which I use to write the phonetic transcriptions in this book. Unfortunately, however, just like video formats, computer systems and measuring systems, the world has not agreed so far to use one and only one phonetic alphabet, with the result that almost every pronunciation book and dictionary uses a different system. To illustrate, here is the way several widely used dictionaries transcribe the humble word *beard*:

Oxford Elementary Learners' Dictionary   bɪəd
Longman American English Dictionary   bɪərd
Webster's Collegiate Dictionary   bɪ(ə)rd
Longman Modern English Dictionary   bɪəd

Returning now to our milk-requesting example, let's transcribe it using the list of phonetic symbols on page 142 (please cover the page below if you want to try this yourself).

ACTIVITY

A:

B:

Your transcription may have come out more or less as follows (note that we do not use capital letters or punctuation in phonetic transcription):

2d

A: kæn aɪ hæv sʌm mɔɹ mɪlk pliːz
B: ʃuɹ dʒʌst ə ˈsɛkənd

(Author's data)

It should be possible to read this exchange and produce intelligible English, even if you were an Aymara speaker who did not understand a word of English. The International Phonetics Association has produced a booklet which contains sample transcriptions of numerous languages, and whenever I have students in class whose native language I don't speak I like to read the corresponding piece from the IPA booklet to them, just to see if they can tell me what I said. It invariably works, which attests to the usefulness of the IPA.

However, we must now draw attention to a shortcoming of this transcription, precise though it may appear to be. People don't actually speak that way. I have already mentioned one difference: *some more* was pronounced as *smore*. In addition, *can I have* came out sounding somewhat like *knef*. The above transcription, in other words, is an idealized or formal version of the real utterances. Such a transcription is often called a <u>broad</u>, or <u>phonemic</u> transcription. It transcribes the distinctive sounds of the language one by one, as if the speaker pronounced every word slowly and carefully (the way teachers do, sometimes).

Every language has a relatively small set of sounds that can distinguish meaning, or <u>phonemes</u> (English has forty-four, in most dialects). To establish the set of phonemes of a language, linguists often use sets of minimal pairs, that is, pairs of words that differ only in one sound, for example, *pat* and *bat*, *bat* and *bit*, *sin* and *sing* (the /ŋ/in/sɪŋ/ is one phoneme, even though it is represented by the two letters <u>ng</u>).

Sometimes two sounds in a language can be quite different, yet they may not be two separate phonemes. For instance, the <u>l</u> in *milk* is quite different from the <u>l</u> in *please*: in *milk* it sounds further back in the mouth, in *please* it sounds much nearer the front. To hear this, pronounce both words slowly, and when you get to the <u>l</u>, hold it and lengthen it. The <u>l</u> in *milk* is called a dark l (or [ɫ]), and the <u>l</u> in *please* is called a 'clear' l. Although these sounds are quite different, there are no words in English in which replacing one <u>l</u> with the other would change the meaning of the word. In this case, the two l's are not separate phonemes, but they are both **allophones** of one phoneme: /l/. Actually, in some dialects, for example, in London, *milk* might be pronounced as '*miwk*', and that particular sound is then also an allophone of /l/.

This is probably enough technical language for the moment. However, the issue of phonemes and allophones can be quite important in learning foreign languages, particularly for speakers who aspire to native-like pronunciation. As an example, I once heard an announcer of a classical music programme on the radio whose English was flawless. Until he used the word *all*, at which point I said to myself: I bet he's German. Sure enough, when the credits were read later, this turned out to be true. The only thing that gave the speaker away, for me at least, was the l in *all*: it was a clear l rather than the dark l which English speakers use after vowels.

ACTIVITY

While pronouncing the following pairs of words, try to spot an allophonic difference in the underlined sounds:

2e

	A	B
1.	key	cold
2.	top	stop
3.	inline	incline
4.	butt	butter
5.	hat	bad

(Author's data)

In general terms, one characteristic of spoken language is that the sounds adapt to each other, changing slightly to make the transition to the next sound (or from the previous sound) easier, blending into one another, or even disappearing altogether. This process is called **assimilation**, and every language has characteristic patterns of sound linking, levelling and loss, often called absorption patterns. In a sense, we want to make speaking as easy as possible, and the more similar a sound is to the ones around it, the easier.

On the other hand, if we make things too easy, we will run into problems of intelligibility: people will simply not understand us and tell us to stop mumbling and to speak clearly. One of the most interesting facets of spoken language is this inherent tension between maximum clarity and ease of articulation. Every language, and every speaker, will find their own balance, teachers erring on one side, perhaps, and people who've had a few beers, on the other.

The last level of sound on our triangle is that of the syllable, one of the most important and trickiest aspects of spoken language. Even though it doesn't fit very easily into the pyramid (hence it has been patched on to it), I feel obliged to give some attention to it. There is currently a great deal of interest in the syllable, hard to define though it is, since it appears to be a key element in many respects, including speech processing and production. One factor in this involves the permitted combinations and sequences of sounds in a language, or the **phonotactics**. For example, English allows the combination initial s + stop (or plosive), st, sp, sk, as in *steep*, *spot*, *sky*. Spanish, however, does not allow this combination, and as a result Spanish learners of English say things like estop, espot, and eschool. Note that, historically speaking, many European languages had problems with this initial cluster in Latin. In French, *scola* became *école*, in German it became *Schule*, or /ʃula/, in Spanish, *escuela*. There are thus powerful constraints against certain sound combinations in certain languages, and language learners tend to have great difficulty in learning sound combinations that their native language does not allow.

2.1.2 Stress and intonation: saying and comprehending

The syllable also relates closely to the **stress** and the rhythm of language. In English we can observe that stressed syllables alternate with unstressed syllables in regular patterns. This is easy to illustrate with nursery rhymes:

HICK ory DICK ory DOCK
the MOUSE ran UP the CLOCK

In English, utterances tend to have one or more 'peaks' of stressed syllables interspersed with unstressed syllables. The time between peaks tends to be roughly constant regardless of the number of syllables that intervene. You can try this out by saying the following utterances while tapping on 'fax' and 'now' each time:

2f

fax		*now*
fax it		*now*
fax it right		*now*
fax it to me		*now*

(Author's data)

In this respect English is different from many other languages, such as Spanish, Finnish and Japanese, in which syllables last a similar amount of time, and no vowels are reduced. Languages like English are called stress-timed, and languages like Spanish are called syllable-timed. One result of this difference is that students of English often say that English speakers 'swallow half of their words'. Conversely, I have heard learners of Spanish complain that Spanish speakers speak incredibly fast, and learners of Finnish sometimes say that Finnish 'sounds like a machine gun: rat-tat-tat-tat-tat.'

Finally, in the realm of sound, we need to consider the issue of **intonation**, or variations of pitch in utterances. In our example, the request for milk ends in a rising intonation, whereas the response has a falling intonation on both parts:

2g

A: Can I have some more milk, please?

B: Sure, just a second.
(Author's data)

It is interesting that the first utterance is perceived as one unit (tone unit), and the second as two. We can say the first utterance also as two units, like this:

2h

A: Can I have some more milk?   Please?
(Author's data)

In which case the request obtains a pleading, begging quality. It is clear that intonation is used to convey a speaker's attitude to what is said. In general, a rising intonation is perceived as being more polite than a falling one which, especially in requests, will be perceived as bossy, or even rude.

The **sociolinguist** John Gumperz (_Discourse Strategies_ 1982) found, when doing research in London, that native-English speaking bus conductors tended to say utterances like the following with a kind of sing-song intonation:

2i

Exact change, please!
(Author's data)

whereas Indian or Pakistani conductors tended to use a falling intonation, as follows:

2j

Exact change, please!
(Gumperz 1982)

The latter may be perceived as pushy and rude by passengers, and can lead to friction or arguments. The above example shows how important minute differences in language use can be, and how language awareness can be of benefit in everyday situations.

Intonation can also create differences in meaning that go beyond attitudinal information. Try to read the following examples according to the suggested intonation patterns, and see if a difference in meaning suggests itself:

2k

A: I didn't get the job because of my husband.

_____/\\/\

B: I didn't get the job because of my husband.

(Author's data)

In the first case, the speaker did not get the job, because her husband messed things up. In the second case, she did get the job, but her husband could not claim any credit for the achievement.

2.2 Morphemes and word-building

We now leave the realm of sound and move on to form. The first unit we encounter here is the unit **morpheme**. Morphemes are the smallest units of language that carry meaning (phonemes may distinguish meaning, but are in themselves meaningless: we cannot say what /p/ or /z/ mean). Some morphemes can stand by themselves, for example, *song*, *fork*, *table*, and *elephant*, others can only be attached to other morphemes, for example, *pre-*, *dis-*, *-ing*, *-s*. The former are called 'free' morphemes, the latter 'bound' morphemes (or **affixes**). You may wonder what meaning a tiny morpheme like *-s* could possibly have. Well, in English it means plural when it's attached to a noun (three *bears*, many *trees*), or third-person subject when it's added to a verb in the present tense (she *sings*, he *dances*).

In most languages words can be made up by putting two or more morphemes together, though some use this device more than others. Analytical languages (Chinese, Vietnamese, English) use it less, synthetic languages (German, Turkish, Aymara) use it more (further distinctions among language types, such as isolating, agglutinative and fusional, criss-cross and overlap according to various features, for example, the extent to which grammatical inflections

25

are used, or morphemes are blended together, changing their
original form when they are combined; see Edward Sapir, *Language*
1921).

English is considered a relatively analytical language, though
there is a fair amount of <u>compounding</u> (combining free morphemes)
and <u>derivation</u> (combining free and bound morphemes). Some
compounds are so well-established that they form one word, written
together, such as *bookcase, keyboard, notebook*. In such cases, the
stress is invariably on the first part (compare, for example, *blackbird*
– a type of bird – to *black bird* – any bird that is black). Other
compounds that haven't been around as long, or that are used less
frequently, may be hyphenated, for example, *beta-test* (as in 'I
beta-test a lot of software'), *in-depth*, and *world-class*. Finally,
words may be habitually combined into **collocations**, or just put
together for the occasion. The area of compounding can thus be
seen as a continuum from 'tight' to 'loose', as follows:

2I

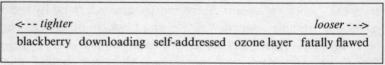

(Author's data)

Another common way of putting words together is by derivation,
a process in which free and bound morphemes are combined. As
an example, the free morpheme *use* can be combined with a
number of bound morphemes:

2m

Prefixes	Suffixes	Both
misuse	useful(ness)	unuseable
disuse	useless(ness)	non-user
over-use	useability	abusive

(Author's data)

Derivational morphemes may have a special function, for example to make a verb out of a noun or an adjective, or a noun out of a verb. In addition, they may have a special meaning, for example, the meaning of *un-* is 'the opposite' (of whatever follows it, such as *undo, ungrateful, unbirthday*). The following little exercise illustrates some functions and meanings of common derivational morphemes (the first example has been completed).

ACTIVITY

2n

Base word	Word + morpheme	Function	Meaning
1 work	work-er	verb to noun	agent
2 red	red-(d)en		(or agentive)
3 danger	en-danger		
4 idol	idol-ize		
5 read	read-able		

(Author's data)

Not all morphemes conform to this neat and regular pattern. In this as in other cases, no sooner do we spot a straightforward pattern, than the quirky and anarchic side of language begins to stir, as if saying to us, 'Hey, don't think I am dull and predictable: anything goes with me!' Here are a few examples of unruly language:

2o

— *What's the difference between a* <u>*terminator*</u> *and an* <u>*ex-terminator?*</u>
— *What is* <u>*season-able*</u> *(or* <u>*un-season-able*</u>, *for that matter) weather?*
— *If* <u>*idolize*</u> *means making an idol out of someone, why does* <u>*burglarize*</u> *not mean making a burglar out of someone?*
— *Is* <u>*flammable*</u> *different from* <u>*inflammable?*</u>

(Author's data)

Samuel Johnson, the famous eighteenth-century pioneer of dictionaries, said it well:

To our language may be with great justness applied the observation of Quintilian, that speech was not formed by an analogy sent from heaven. It did not descend to us in a state of uniformity and perfection, but was produced by necessity and enlarged by accident, and is therefore composed of dissimilar parts, thrown together by negligence, by affectation, by learning, or by ignorance. (quoted in Yule, *The Study of Language* (1985), page 59).

2.2.1 Affixes – followers of fashion

One of the things that affects the slapping of morphemes on to morphemes is fashion. In fact, the eminent American linguist Dwight Bolinger has called some bound morphemes (also called affixes – divided into prefixes, suffixes, and infixes) 'fashion-fixes'.

He quoted the example of *out-*, as in *outperform*, *outdo*, etc. Indeed, some time ago I saw a magazine cover announcing that Korea might 'out-Japan Japan'. Currently it seems that the prefix *pre-* is much in fashion. A recent movie trailer had an eager young employee saying to his boss: 'I'd like to pre-apologize for anything I have done or might do in the future.' In addition to this humorous example, we have the following derived forms with *pre-*:
— pre-used (cars)
— pre-recorded (tapes)
— pre-loved (carpets; why does the image of a fireplace come to mind as well?)
— pre-owned (Mercedes; perhaps pre-admired, or pre-pampered would be even better)
— preplan (this is redundant: *plan* already presupposes *pre-*, otherwise it would be something done before planning)
— precooked (meals; cooked before you <u>buy</u> them. Most meals are [pre-?] cooked before you <u>eat</u> them)
— pre-approved (loans; in one commercial a loan was offered for which you could, tautologously, be 'pre-approved in advance').
— On flights, passengers with small children may pre-board (other airline talk includes *re-stowing* your luggage under your seat, and *deplaning* once the aircraft has come to a complete stop).

Like spiders (or visiting relatives), morphemes seem to turn up in unexpected and sometimes even unwanted places. Once they are there, however, they may spin a web of familiarity, and we may come to regard their presence as natural, or even cease to pay them any attention.

2.3 The word and its definitions

We now turn our attention to the next level: the word. A number of different kinds of words can be seen in our example, words like *milk*, *sure* and *second*, and words like *can, I*, and *a*:

2b (repeat)

A: *Can I have some more milk, please?*
B: *Sure, just a second.*

Some of these words carry more meaning than others. The two most important words, in terms of information load, are probably *milk* and *sure*. In fact, we can leave all the other words out, and the exchange might still work:

2p

A: *Milk?*
B: *Sure.*
(Author's data)

We can't do that so easily with any other pair of words in the exchange, for example, *A: Have? B: Just*. Some other combinations might work, for example, *A: Some more? B: A second*.

Playing around with language in this way, it becomes clear that different words, or groups of words (called <u>constituents</u>) have different **functions**. Words that carry most of the information content (nouns, verbs, adjectives, adverbs) are often called <u>content</u> words, and 'little words' that function mainly to connect, organize and direct attention (pronouns, articles, prepositions etc) are often called <u>function</u> words. We can leave out all or most of the function words, and our message may still make sense. In fact, this is often done in newspaper headlines:

RECORD HEAT ENGULFS BAY AREA
GANG VIOLENCE GETTING WORSE

In cases such as the above it is quite easy to fill in the missing function words. However, this is not always the case. Students of English (and perhaps some native speakers as well) might find headlines such as the following quite puzzling:

PARED CHARGES MUDDLE ALTMAN CASE
JAPAN CUTS ROT FROM CLEAN IMAGE

The word is traditionally regarded as the central unit of language. As the Gospel of St. John puts it: 'In the beginning was the Word.' The great linguist Edward Sapir (whose book *Language* is still well worth reading, even though it was published in 1921) noted the centrality of the word, but also showed that it is very hard to give a clear definition of it:

The best that we can do is to say that the word is one of the smallest, completely satisfying bits of isolated 'meaning' into which the sentence resolves itself. It cannot be cut into without a disturbance of meaning, one or the other or both of the severed parts remaining as a helpless waif on our hands. (page 34).

From an analytical perspective, every word can be said to have four basic aspects: sound, form, **syntax**, and meaning (-s), as represented in the following diagram:

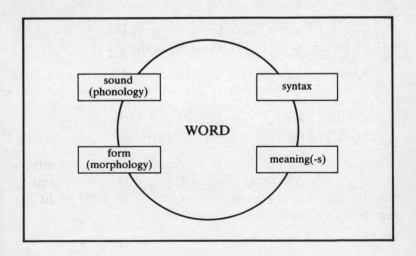

To put this in perspective, to 'know' a word means knowing at least four kinds of things:
— how to pronounce it (the sounds and the way they are combined);
— how it is made up of parts (syllables, morphemes, other words);
— how it combines with other words in phrases and sentences;
— the different things it can mean.

If we are literate, we may have a fifth type of knowledge: how to write the word. Further, we might add a sixth type of knowledge, which we might call social or pragmatic knowledge: when it is appropriate to use the word, whether it is considered polite or rude, etc. I would argue, however, that these last two knowledge types are fringe issues, although in some circles they may carry great weight (for example, spelling bees are quite an institution in the US, but I have never heard of a pronouncing bee or a grammar bee).

ACTIVITY

2q
The following exercise illustrates the different kinds of knowledge we have (rather, may have) of words (the spelling is already given):

Word	Pronunciation	Morphology	Syntax	Meaning	Pragmatics
often	ɔfən / ɔftən	2 syllables, stress on first	adverb, before or after verb	regularly, many times	ɔftən is less common, sounds more formal
give			verb, usually takes two objects, direct and indirect		
alligator		one morpheme, four syllables			
shit					taboo, but quite common in Hollywood movies
peckish					
liposuction					

(Author's data)

Words in a sentence have to be said one after the other, and their order is, in English at least, crucial. *John loves Mary* is quite different from *Mary loves John*. The most common word order in English is SVO (Subject + Verb + Object), with other sentence constituents draped around these key parts in various ways. Of course, when forming questions, we may put a verb in front of the subject, as was the case in our example:

Can I have some more milk, please?
 Vf S Vnf   Od   Adv

Here, Vf means Finite Verb, and Vnf means Non-finite (or infinite) Verb (S means Subject, and Od means Direct Object). The former means a verb form that is marked for tense (*can* or *could*) and agreement (which does not show on auxiliary verbs like *can*, but does show on verbs like *be: am - is - are*). The non-finite verb is usually the main verb, in the infinitive or participle (he has *worked*, she will *study*, it is *raining*). Other sentence elements, like adverbs (Adv, above), prepositional phrases and relative clauses, can be added in various places, with greater or lesser flexibility of movement. Try and see which parts in the following sentences can be moved without changing the meaning in any substantial way.

ACTIVITY

2r

— *But I did the dishes yesterday.*
— *Not all my socks have holes in them.*
— *I think I'll travel to Chiclayo next month, if I get the money.*
— *Last week I saw a raccoon in our backyard.*
(Author's data)

From the above it should be clear that in any utterance or sentence words have to follow one another in some order and grouping that is systematic. This order and grouping cannot usually be changed without changing the meaning, or without making the utterance or sentence ungrammatical.

The ways in which words follow one another and are related to one another is called the syntagmatic dimension of language, the dimension of 'chaining' or sequencing. At every slot, or link in the chain, there may be other words that can be chosen to fill that slot, creating a second dimension of language, that of choice, or the paradigmatic dimension, as follows:

2s

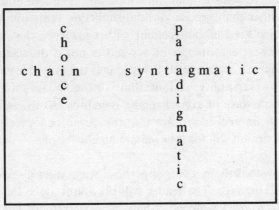

(Author's data)

Let's try this on one of our utterances:

2t

May	you	get	lots	less	coffee,	
Can	**I**	**have**	**some**	**more**	**milk,**	**please?**
Should	she	request	a little		Chardonnay?	
1	2	3	4	5	6	7

(Author's data)

You will notice that you cannot choose freely which words to 'slot' into the different places in the chain. In some places (especially 2 and 6) you are freer than in others. What are the kinds of rules that constrain your choices, and how do these rules relate to those that constrain the chaining? These questions have occupied linguists for generations and, in some formulation or other, the tentative answers form the backbone of most linguistic theories. Without going into any theoretical discussions, I recommend that you play around with the chaining and choosing a little to become aware of both the constraints and the creativity that the interplay, or the 'meshing', of these dimensions bring to language.

All along, remember that this meshing is rough and rather anarchic, rather than precise and tightly fitting. This roughness of fit is not some kind of shortcoming of language, in the same way that the criss-cross looseness of a weed is not a drawback to its ability to overrun a backyard. Rather, it is actually the key to the extraordinary versatility and flexibility of language, and to its resilience in the face of ever-changing demands. At the same time, however, this imprecision means that the quest for a precise grammatical description will for ever remain an elusive one.

We have now looked, in a very superficial way, at a tiny part of the structure of language. The reader will no doubt agree that we are dealing with a very complex system here, or rather, a system of systems. Using the word system, I am thinking more of an ecosystem, such as a rain forest or a wetland, and less of some kind of machine with predetermined operations and rules, like a four-stroke engine. Understanding a rain forest is quite a different proposition to understanding a well-oiled machine, and I would propose that the understanding of language is much more like the former than the latter.

In view of the complexity, and at times the unruliness, of language, it is no wonder that one frequently meets people who say that they have taken several courses in this or that language, but have given up in despair. It also explains why children who are thrown into a situation in which a foreign language is communicatively necessary, suffer enormous amounts of stress and frustration (the 'effortless' acquisition of a second language by children is nothing but a myth: children in such situations crucially need the back-up and security of their native language, their mother tongue). It further casts extreme doubt upon the veracity of the ubiquitous advertisements for programmes which claim to teach a foreign language in a few weeks without studying. We will return to the issue of language learning in chapter 6.

We have now looked at language in terms of sounds, words,

sentences, and other units. But there is of course much more to language than such an atomistic description of bits and pieces. In fact, the reader may reasonably object that so far we have said little of real interest about everyday language use. It is as if we have described a game of chess by saying: I see a number of pieces of different shapes, made of wood, with bits of green felt on the bottom, standing in different positions on a square flat piece of chequered wood. It is time, therefore, to go to the 'game' itself, and explore its meaning and purpose.

PROJECT

The best way to do formal linguistic analysis is to work with a text or data that you have collected yourself: a **conversation** you have recorded and transcribed, a commercial recorded from TV, a newspaper article, a song, ads from magazines and so on. Here are some suggested topics:
— Brand names for sweets, cereals etc.
— Ways of saying winning/losing on TV sports broadcasts (creamed, edged past etc — this may work best in the US)
— Comparing word formation in two languages
— Description of intonation patterns
— A conversation between two students about a forthcoming test
— Compliments and responses to compliments in cross-cultural encounters
— The use of tag questions compared between males and females
— The structure of recorded telephone messages

SUMMARY

- A critical awareness of language requires a basic knowledge of how language is put together.
- The relationship between the spoken and written word is not identical in all languages: it may be more or less transparent or opaque.

- Traditionally language is divided into various units, such as phonemes, morphemes, words, phrases, clauses, sentences and texts.
- Prosodic or suprasegmental features (stress, rhythm, intonation) provide a great deal of information, for example, about the speaker's attitude concerning the message.
- Knowing a word means the combination of several different kinds of knowledge, including its pronunciation and spelling, its morphology, its grammatical connections and its pragmatic range of uses.
- Word order is fairly strict in English, more so than in many other languages.

3 Context and interpretation

The description in chapter 2 has hinted at complex systems of knowledge that speakers of a language must possess in order to express their intentions and interpret those of others. In order to investigate how we can 'make meaning' by using language, it is necessary to bring in the notion of context, that is, the way the various elements are combined, how they relate to the world at large, and the purposes for which they are used. This side of language study is generally called **pragmatics**. The central message of pragmatics is that meaning does not come ready-made or 'packaged' in words or sentences, but is constructed by speakers and hearers through processes of interpretation, in the context in which the language is used.

In this chapter, I will distinguish three levels (or layers) of context:

— the linguistic context, or the ways in which the various units discussed in chapter 2 are combined;

— the interactional context, or the ways in which people's utterances are organized and follow one another in a regular manner;

— the social context, or the ways in which institutional, socio-economic, cultural and political considerations influence and are influenced by the verbal actions of people.

These layers are depicted in concentric circles on the diagram on the next page with which we will begin our discussion.

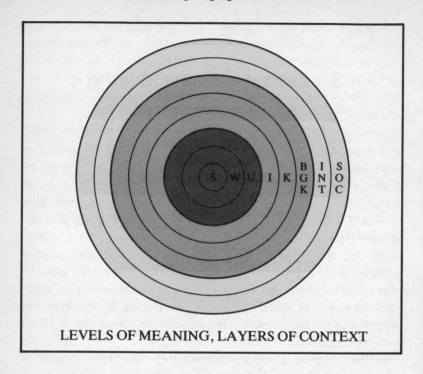

LEVELS OF MEANING, LAYERS OF CONTEXT

3.1 Levels of meaning, layers of context

One can look at the context of language as a series of concentric circles with the actual language use at the centre. One such series of concentric circles would be the hierarchical set of linguistic units we talked about in the last chapter. We can add to it the broader, more global aspects of paralinguistics, such as intonation (including, for the sake of convenience, stress and rhythm under this heading; this group of features is often called **prosodic** or **suprasegmental** features), **kinesics**, or body language, and background knowledge. Beyond that we add the layers of interactional and social context. We thus end up with a multi-layered interpretive framework, in which all layers contribute to the meaning (the speaker's intention and the hearer's interpretation) of an utterance, but there is not one single layer that contains the essence of the meaning (note that we are talking about spoken language only; written language has developed its own set of adapted structural features, which we will only briefly address in this book). Metaphorically speaking, the meaning is a bit like an onion: we can peel off the layers one by one, but we should not expect to get at the heart or the core of the onion eventually: when we have peeled off all the layers, the onion is gone.

Let's explore the layers of interpretation by looking at some examples for each one. The easiest way to illustrate how meaning-making operates, is to examine examples of miscommunication or ambiguity.

S – sound:

patios – pantyhose This example is taken from a TV commercial for a pizza chain, in which a 'godfather-type', chewing on a fat cigar, reminisced about the good life, involving – apart from pizzas, of course – big houses, swimming pools, and *patios*. A colleague of mine expressed puzzlement at the inclusion of *pantyhose* among the good things in life. Although the two words are apparently quite different, in a certain nasalized, cigar-chomping pronunciation, they can actually sound quite similar. Hence the confusion.

W – word:

embarrassed – embarazada This is the classic tale of the American woman visiting Mexico and spilling her taco all over her dress. She wants to say that she is *embarrassed*, but actually says that she is pregnant (*Estoy embarazada*). *Embarrassed* and *embarazada* are so-called false cognates, that is, they look similar but mean different things. I committed an example of lexical miscommunication during a recent visit to Japan, where I was asked by a class of English students what some popular foods were in California. One of the items I mentioned was

41

tacos, and I was somewhat surprised and relieved (for not having to explain what I meant) to see the students nodding in comprehension. It was explained to me afterwards that *tako* means octopus in Japanese. As a result, there is now a group of young Japanese people who believe that octopus is the favourite food of Californians.

U – utterance (or clause/sentence in written language):

A nice example of this is Chomsky's famous sentence: *Visiting aunts can be boring.* This sentence can mean either that aunts who come to visit may bore you, or that going to visit aunts can be a boring activity. Another example is a recent headline in a newspaper, probably penned somewhat tongue-in-cheek by the reporter, that YELTSIN WANTS RUSSIANS TO BE MORE REVOLTING.

These three layers complete what is usually known as core linguistics, the traditional field of study of linguists. Courses of formal language study tend to concentrate on sounds, words and sentences, with 'proper' pronunciation, a large vocabulary (and 'proper' spelling), and 'correct' grammar being the overriding, if not exclusive, concerns of teachers and examiners. One of the purposes of language awareness is to show that a living language education goes far beyond such a narrow, prescriptive focus. Let us therefore continue worming our way outwards through the next layer of the diagram.

I – intonation:

As I mentioned in the previous chapter, one of the prime functions of intonation is to provide information about the speaker's attitude and emotions. This is of course an oversimplification, as the example I quoted there shows: *I didn't get the job because of my husband.* A similar example would be: *I'm not going to trust anybody,* in a falling versus a rise-fall-rise intonation on the word *anybody.* To reveal more closely the attitudinal aspect of intonation, the reader might like to practise different ways of saying yes.

ACTIVITY

3a

Yees!	*(enthusiastic)*
Yes.	*(matter-of-fact)*
Yeeees-	*(hesitating)*
Yeeees?	*(I don't think so)*
Yeess??	*(no!)*

(Author's data)

K – kinesics:

Sometimes our gestures, facial expression, or posture belie the words we say. Parents in this way determine whether their children are telling the truth or not. Some kinesic features may be involuntary, such as blushing, fidgeting and sweating, and we may call this type of behaviour the 'Pinocchio's nose' effect. Other kinesic features may be deliberate and controlled. When we grow up we may learn to control those kinesic behaviours that gave us away as children: we may even learn to tell the most bald-faced lies while remaining cool as cucumbers. An example of kinesic behaviour that contradicts the more literal aspects of the message occurs frequently at cocktail parties, especially if some of the dignitaries have sampled the refreshments rather liberally. At some point, while listening to someone droning on about their golf game or how to breed perfect dachshunds, you may well say, 'How interesting!' while rolling your eyes so that a friend, standing near by, understands that you mean: 'How boring!' As is the case with other features, for example, with intonation, it is worth pointing out that there is a great deal of cultural variation in kinesic markers. For example, eye contact while talking may indicate sincerity in one culture, but not in another.

BGK – background knowledge:

Let's say you need a new car, and you sit down with your spouse to discuss which one to buy. The following exchange takes place:

> *Spouse: Let's get a BMW.*
> *You: Sure, we're rolling in money.*

In this case, our background knowledge tells us that you mean we are not rolling in money, and that buying a BMW would be an act of irresponsible extravagance, and is therefore out of the question. We would probably arrive at this interpretation even if you did not signal your displeasure with a sarcastic tone of voice or a sardonic smile.

This completes the second set of layers of suprasegmental (or prosodic) features, kinesics and background knowledge. From here we move into the wider circles of the **interactional** and the social contexts. At the interactional level we must consider such things as taking turns, signalling attention, showing and being shown respect, controlling and being controlled, and so on. At the social (including social, societal, cultural, human) level of context, an even broader range of factors come into play, including such things as group identity, dominance, professional **discourse worlds**, world views, and so on. The following examples merely give a brief glimpse of the interpretive processes involved.

INT – interactional:

At the interactional level, participants are concerned with taking turns, hearing each other, showing that they are 'on the same wavelength', and so on. A nice example of a play on interactional concerns is the famous contract-signing scene in the Marx Brothers movie *A Night at the Opera*. Here is an excerpt:

Chico: *What does it say?*
Groucho: *Well, go on and read it.*
Chico: *All right – you read it.*
Groucho: *All right – I'll read it to you.*
               Can you hear?
Chico: *I haven't heard anything yet.*
               Did you say anything?
Groucho: *Well, I haven't said anything worth hearing.*
Chico: *Well, that's why I didn't hear anything.*
Groucho: *Well, that's why I didn't say anything.*

SOC – social:

ACTIVITY

Study the following exchange, well-known from the sociolinguistic literature (Ervin-Tripp, from *Sociolinguistics* 1972, page 225), and describe the two participants (in terms of job, race etc), and your guesses as to when and where you think this incident took place. Then reflect on the basis for your judgements.

3b
A: *What's your name, boy?*
B: *Dr Poussaint. I'm a physician.*
A: *What's your first name, boy?*
B: *Alvin.*
(Author's data)

As anyone familiar with American culture will probably have guessed, A is white, and B is African-American. A major clue here is the use of the word *boy* as a term of address to an adult male, and the fact that neither B's last name nor his profession are considered relevant information. Furthermore, as Poussaint informs us, it turns out that A is a policeman, who can thus be seen to be exercising his socially mandated control over an ordinary citizen. The incident took place in the sixties somewhere in the Southern US.

Having worked our way through the concentric circles, let's now stand back and look at the model in a holistic way, to see what it may tell us about the processes of intending and interpreting.

First, the model demonstrates in a dramatic fashion that language use is not a matter of assembling bits and pieces of language, lining them up and constructing a message cumulatively. It seems rather that we start out with meanings, and represent them with the signs of language. Ideas or thoughts are presented to the world (or that part of it which appears to be in communicative contact with us) in the shape of language. They can also be presented in other ways of course, sometimes more effectively. A dancer who was interviewed on TV was asked to say what she tried to express in a particular dance. Her reply was quite apt: 'If I could say it, I wouldn't have to dance it.' Most often, however, our main vehicle for communicating with the world around us, and even with ourselves in the activity called thinking, is language.

In producing an utterance, speakers design it with an audience in mind; after all, we want to be understood the way we want to be understood. 'Please don't let me be misunderstood!' as the old blues song puts it. In other words, we want to make sure that the intentions, attitudes and relations that we wish to convey are indeed conveyed effectively. This includes effectively hiding those intentions, etc, that we prefer to keep hidden from view.

We turn now to the interpretation of utterances. As above, we do not go about this job by assembling the sounds we hear into words, the words into sentences, and so on. Rather, the concentric circles are like a bar-code, and we run the laser pen of our attention across it, registering the meanings that are encoded on the different layers. However, we do not read every layer with the same amount of attention, we focus on those which signal something new, different, or unexpected. We pay particular attention if the information on one layer clashes with that on another.

As experienced language users engaging largely in familiar activities, we are able, on the basis of few clues, to <u>predict</u> much of what will be said next. The more familiar we are with the speaker, the topic, the setting and so on, the less energy we need to spend on scrutinizing all the layers, one by one. If we walk down the same corridor every morning and say 'good morning' to the same people we pass there, then it is unlikely that they would notice it if we changed our message to 'you moron' or 'you're boring'. If, however, we glared ominously instead of smiling in the usual friendly manner, then our colleagues might well take notice. This means that the layers can carry different informational loads.

It is of special interest to note that, if there is any conflict between two adjacent layers, the outer one will in general determine the interpretation. As we saw in chapter 2, the bus conductor's *Exact change, please!* may be interpreted as pushy and rude if said in a falling intonation, even though it includes the word *please*. If, referring to the BMW example, I say *We have lots of money*, my listener's background knowledge will lead to an interpretation in direct contradiction to the sentence, the words and the sounds. In general, then, the outer layers influence overall interpretation more than the inner ones. This is curious, if we consider that in language teaching the inner layers (especially the three 'core' layers) have generally dominated lessons, materials, and teaching practices, often to the utter neglect of the outer layers. Meaningful learning, therefore, would hardly seem possible within a traditional grammar approach. Learning an abundance of grammatical facts, and amassing a vast vocabulary, do not prepare a language learner adequately for real communication, since in a specific context the most important clues may be missed because they are 'unreadable'. Learning to read contextual clues, and to <u>design</u> such clues effectively into one's own messages, are skills that are learned through participating in meaningful events, and through becoming keenly aware of all the things that are given social and cultural meaning in the particular society in which we find ourselves.

3.1.1 Interaction

How are we going to tackle the description of interaction between people? Let's begin by recycling our brief milk-requesting exchange, and look at it as if it were the first time we see it.

2b
A: *Can I have some more milk, please?*
B: *Sure, just a second.*

ACTIVITY

At this point, write a one-paragraph narrative that puts the exchange into a specific context, describing participants (age, relationship), place, time of day, and actions:

We will leave the narrative in the above box alone for the moment (I will come back to it in a while), and look at the interaction in some detail.

First of all, we note that there are two people involved. The language is therefore <u>dialogic</u> rather than <u>monologic</u>, and this means that one utterance is in some way linked to (influenced by, and influences) the other.

Next, we see that the participants **take turns** at speaking so that they can hear each other and accomplish what they want in an orderly manner.

Thirdly, the two utterances share a special relationship, in that the first one is a request and the second a response (or acceptance). Utterances that are related in such ways are called adjacency pairs, other examples being question and answer, greeting and greeting, statement and comment, and so on.

Further, the participants follow certain common-sense principles and regularities (conventions), such as the assumption that the other person is cooperative; economy of expression, that is, saying as much as is required, but not more; clarity, being sufficiently but not overly courteous; and so on. Such things, which we might call a tacit speaker–hearer contract, have been studied under the general name of conversational logic in a highly influential paper by the philosopher Paul Grice. He proposed that conversation is governed by a basic cooperative principle, with various maxims: quality, quantity, relation, and manner. The linguist Geoffrey Leech later proposed an additional maxim: the maxim of tact. Finally, the exchange forms a sort of small 'story', or speech event, which might go something like this:

3c

A family is sitting at the breakfast table. A (a four-year old boy) has just finished his glass of milk and asks for more. B (his mother) finishes putting some marmalade on her toast, then gets up and fetches the bottle of milk from the fridge . . .
(Author's data)

Return now for a moment to the box above and compare the version you wrote (or imagined) with the one presented here. Are there any differences or similarities? The point of this exercise is that we can all, on the basis of a few clues, conjure up a story in which the clues fit. The reason for this is that our knowledge is stored in our memory in the form of stories, scripts, frames, or schemas (all terms used by different cognitive scientists) that represent typical events and experiences in our life. These organizational packages allow us to economize on the effort of interpreting what goes on in the world. Many frequent routines are so well-rehearsed that we need very few clues to know how to deal with them. These may include depositing a cheque at the bank, going to a restaurant, greeting the people at work and many others. Of course, this kind of knowledge, while it makes our daily life a lot easier, also has its risks, namely, that we may fail to notice changes, or are unable to adapt to changing scripts, in other words, too much reliance on ready-made anticipatory stories or schemas may reduce our awareness of what is going on and our flexibility in dealing with the unexpected. In effect, a successfully adapted person will be able to switch from routine performance to vigilance by quickly judging subtle clues in the environment. In a conversation we make these quick, subtle judgements all the time, often without being aware of them.

Our dealings with the world of events thus run the gamut from bewildered incomprehension to robot-like automation, with vigilance and skilled performance at different places along the continuum. Language, and language learning, play a key role in organizing our activities in the world.

3.1.2 Conversation

ACTIVITY

Study the following conversation and think about what the participants are doing.

(the context is: Going on a Bike Ride; for readers not familiar with this kind of transcription, underlining means emphasis, colons mean lengthening, numbers in brackets refer to pauses in seconds, the = sign refers to absence of pause between turns).

3d
1 *A: What time you wanna lea:ve.*
2   *(0.3)*
3 *B: ((smack)) Uh:: sick clo:ck?*
4   *(0.5)*
5 *A: Six (uh) clo:ck? hh =*
6 *B: = Is that good.*
(Schegloff 1984)

However modest and pedestrian this little snippet of talk may appear, close inspection reveals intense interpretive activity and a constant negotiation of meaning. This interpretation and negotiation does not primarily refer to the establishment of a mutually acceptable departure time, but rather to such issues as 'not appearing pushy or bossy', 'sounding tentative', and 'being flexible'. We constantly convey such information about ourselves and receive it from others about them, and this kind of conversational work, related to the phenomena Erving Goffman (1981) called 'footing', requires great precision across all the layers of our interpretive circle (see page 40), and close attention to what we say and hear. Hesitations, smacks, sighs, uh's etc, are by no means to be written off as mere problems of fluency, blemishes, or performance phenomena, rather, they play a crucial role in the negotiation of meanings about ourselves and others. Once again, we see that using language in context is rather remote from the sorts of things contained in grammar books and dictionaries.

Extending this argument, let's look again at our milk-requesting text. If instead of a four-year-old boy and his mother we had a situation as shown in the picture below, what conclusions would we draw?

3e

(Author's data)

One of the possible conclusions here would be that A is a man who expects to be served by the woman, in spite of the fact that the milk is closer to him than it is to her. The exchange thus expresses a relationship of power, and this changes with the participants, their relations, the location of the bottle of milk, and so on. It may also change in accordance with cultural norms and customs. For example, in the above picture, a number of different responses are imaginable, all of them implying different relationships of power, of customs, of familiarity, and so on:

3f

A: Can I have some more milk, please?
B1: Of course, help yourself.
B2: It's right in front of your nose.
B3: No, I have to save some for the baby.

B4: Get it yourself. Can't you see I'm busy?
B5: I'm so sorry, I didn't see your glass was empty.
(Author's data)

And if we make the bottle of milk disappear from the table, we can add yet other scenarios, for example:

B6: Sorry, we don't do free refills of milk.

We can see then that the simple matter of asking for something requires an awesome amount of knowledge in addition to the nouns, verbs, and so on, including knowledge of actual and potential power relationships, knowledge about 'the way things are done around here', and much more. In our original example of the four-year-old, this would include the knowledge that he is considered too small to get up and get the heavy gallon jug of milk from the fridge himself, and the knowledge to be polite and use 'the magic word "please."'

Considerations such as these have led philosophers of language, sociologists, anthropologists and others, to regard conversation as one of the most basic of all human activities, one that is intimately connected with the learning of language, cultural development and the growth of consciousness. Vygotsky, the brilliant Russian psychologist of the early twentieth century, had the following to say about conversation:

In conversation, every sentence is prompted by a motive. Desire or need lead to request, question to answer, bewilderment to explanation. The changing motives of the interlocutors determine at every moment the turn oral speech will take. It does not have to be consciously directed – the dynamic situation takes care of that. (*Thought and Language* (1962), page 99).

Conversation, which ironically so often seems merely relaxation, goofing about, a 'shooting the breeze' in between periods of serious work, turns out to be the human activity which, more than any other, contains in its dynamic unfolding the threads out of which the fabric of social and intellectual life is woven.

If we compare this chapter to chapter 2, we can see that we have looked at language from two perspectives, each one incomplete in itself, both of them complementing one another and adding a few pieces to a complex puzzle. It would be foolish to pretend that our picture is now complete. At best we have begun to see the outlines of a vast and detailed landscape. In this chapter we looked at what it takes to understand and be understood through language. We have seen that the 'nuts and bolts' we identified in chapter 2 are only a small part of the total array of features that play a role in producing and interpreting talk. Equally important are the so-called 'paralinguistic' features of stress, rhythm and intonation, various contextual features and background knowledge. In fact, I proposed the rule that, if an interpretive conflict should arise between two circles, the interpretation suggested by the outer circle is likely to prevail over the interpretation suggested by the inner circle.

In general, both production and interpretation move from the global to the particular rather than the other way around. Schemas, scripts and frames of various kinds allow us to set up predictions by which we are enabled to anticipate to a certain extent what will be said next, or what we are expected to say next. These predictive stores make our dealings with one another much more efficient, although they may also make us less adaptable and less able to notice and deal with changes.

PROJECT

Record a spoken encounter or speech event, or some identifiable episode in a conversation, a lesson, an interview and so on, and transcribe it in detail, trying to make sense of it in the context, identifying purposes and tracing relationships between actions. To do this, consulting one or more of the books recommended on pages 143–146 will be necessary, since our chapter has only given the briefest of overviews. The following steps are useful in a project like this:

1. Identify an area you wish to study (in terms of setting, participants, topic)
2. Record the data on audio or video (the latter especially if non-verbal data are important)
3. Transcribe the encounter, consulting one of the sources on transcription cited. You will find that this is an intensive and time-consuming, but ultimately rewarding job.
4. Look for patterns, such as **speech acts**, adjacency pairs, (sub-)units that appear to be connected, and so on. Here, consulting a book such as Hatch or Nunan will be useful.
5. Analyse the context in terms of a particular model suggested in the literature (again, see Hatch, Nunan, or one of the other books on discourse or context) or devise your own model.
6. Write up the results in the form of a report or paper.

SUMMARY

- The meaning of language is to a large extent determined by its use in actual contexts.
- If the literal message (the 'dictionary meaning') of words and utterances conflicts with the message provided by the context, for example, through kinesics, intonation or body language, the contextual meaning will override the literal meaning.
- Interaction has its own logic, which depends on the principle of cooperation between interlocutors. Even though this principle is often broken in practice, we rely on it to make sense of our interactions.
- Conversation is the most basic, and arguably the most important form of interaction. It is often regarded as the basic vehicle for cultural and social development.

4 Simmering pots of meaning

> P: *Would you agree that I'm talking and you're not talking?*
> D: *Yes, I'm –*
> P: *[You may speak now.*
> D: *Because I can't get a word in edgeways.*
> P: *Oh fine. Well fine. Which – which word would you like to put in?*
> D: *I have no idea . . . perhaps . . .*
> P: *Which – which particular word would you like to put in edgeways? What about edgeways?*
> D: *Maybe I'd like to put the word edgeways in.*
> P: *Put it in. Feel free.*
> D: *Put it on its side, thrust it through, and –*
> P: *[Let it be.*
> D: *And let it be.*
> P: *All right, we've admitted the word edgeways. Where has it got you?*
> D: *[Edgeways.*
> P: *Where has it got you?*
> D: *Where has it got me? Nowhere.*

(Peter Cook and Dudley Moore: *The best of . . . What's left of . . . Not only . . . But also*)

In this chapter we will look a little more closely at meaning. After all, that's what language is all about. Our prime suspect here is the word, since it is the main carrier of meaning. However, when words are put together in various ways, the sum is always more than the parts, so that different combinations of words (sentences or utterances, phrases, expressions, and so on) will also be part of our focus.

Most readers will be familiar with the old proverb:

Sticks and stones may break my bones, but words will never hurt me.

and will agree that this is a valiant attempt to deny the power of words, but that in reality words do hurt, often very much indeed.

And then there is the fact that words can mean a number of different things, with overtones and **connotations**, with literal and figurative senses, all possibly related in some way, but not easy to pin down. This is what led C. S. Lewis to speak of certain words as 'simmering pots of meaning' (*Studies in Words* (1960), page 196).

Not only do words have a range of meanings, these meanings also change, both over time and from place to place and setting to setting. The word *gay* now has a different (or additional, if you prefer) meaning than it had twenty or so years ago. *Computer* has changed from 'someone who makes calculations' to the desktop machine on which I am writing now (and in between, it meant for a while a roomful of equipment looked after by technicians in white coats).

The analysis of words also gives us insight into how our mind operates: how we store and retrieve things, and how language relates to thought.

Finally, we often use one word to mean another, either for purposes of play, or to add a new edge of significance to our expression (as in the case of metaphor).

These are the sorts of things we will be looking at in this chapter. By way of introduction, let's try a little quiz to test your lexical sophistication. In the third column of the table below, write the name of the relationship between the two words in the first two columns. Use terms like the following (see glossary):

— synonym
— antonym
— hyponym
— homophone
— homonym
— converse

shallow	*deep*	*1*
mature	*ripe*	*2*
suite	*sweet*	*3*
table	*furniture*	*4*
single	*married*	*5*
bear (animal)	*bear (carry)*	*6*
move	*run*	*7*
buy	*sell*	*8*
steal	*take*	*9*
stubborn	*obstinate*	*10*

(Author's data)

Some of these pairs you may have found easier to classify than others: 10 is clearly a case of synonyms, with negligible differences in meaning and use, 2 is trickier: although many would call them synonyms, mature and ripe cannot be used interchangeably in many cases (see Bolinger and Sears, *Aspects of Language*, 1981): we can say mature fruit or ripe fruit, but not ripe trees or ripe people (try referring to someone as a 'ripe student' instead of a 'mature student'). For this reason we might call *ripe* a hyponym of *mature* since, although both words share the same basic meaning, *mature* covers all cases, but *ripe* only covers a subset (especially fruit). *Shallow* and *deep* (1) are gradable antonyms, since there are degrees of shallowness and depth. By contrast, a pair like *dead* and *alive* might be considered non-gradable, since 'less dead' or 'more alive' are not normally used (except in metaphorical usage). Many non-gradable antonyms can be called <u>converse</u> terms (also, sometimes, <u>complementary</u>), as in the case of 5: *single* and *married* (everybody is either single or married – though some people might consider *divorced* a third category). *Buying* and *selling* are complementary, since a buying action always presupposes a simultaneous selling action. Which of the following would you consider to be true complementary terms?

ACTIVITY

4c

lend	—	*borrow*
let	—	*rent*
teach	—	*learn*
give	—	*take*
come	—	*go*

(Author's data)

4.1 Connotation

Words have dictionary meanings; they refer to objects, feelings, people, qualities, and so on. These meanings, which remain stable enough to be printed without immediately being out of date, are the denotative meanings of words. In this sense a dog is a certain kind of quadruped mammal, a tree is a tall plant with a woody stem and branches, and happiness is – whatever you want it to be. In addition to these meanings, words may have emotional (positive or negative) meanings associated with them, called connotative meanings. A word like *edgeways* will not have much connotation for most people (except, perhaps, after reading the Pete and Dud extract above), but words like *moron, chocolate* and *marriage* do, for many people, carry significant emotional weight.

The connotations of certain words make us at times look for more neutral alternatives, or more pleasant-sounding synonyms. Such words are called euphemisms. In this way, 'I have to let you go' is supposed to sound less unpleasant than 'You're fired.' Similarly, 'The policemen violated Mr K's civil rights' sounds more civilized than 'The policemen savagely beat an unarmed black man half to death.' On the other side of the coin, people sometimes deliberately use rough and negatively loaded words to shock, to show solidarity with friends, or to express anger or contempt. Such usage, being the opposite of euphemism, is often called dysphemism. So, if we don't the wish to say that Ms So-and-so has dicd, we may use a euphemism and say that she 'passed away', but if we feel less charitably inclined to her memory we might use a dysphemism and say that she 'croaked' or 'kicked the bucket'. As a result, she may be either 'resting in peace' or 'pushing up the daisies'.

Many names or actions can be expressed in neutral terms, euphemistically, or dysphemistically, along a continuum that ranges from 'nice' to 'normal' to 'naughty' (or 'rude'). Thus, *rest room* is nice, *toilet* (or *bathroom*, for those who would regard toilet as being already on the rude side) is normal, and *loo, bog* or *john* are rude (though only mildly so). We might string such a series of words on aline like this (you might add other words, such as *lavatory, comfort room, shithouse*; many words like this are regional):

4d

```
NICE ----------------------NORMAL ----------------------RUDE

powder room – bathroom – men's room – toilet – john – bog – crapper
– rest room – ladies' room – loo – karzey
```

(Author's data)

Such a sliding scale of verbal etiquette can easily be turned into an exercise for students of English and others who wish to learn to vary their register both up and down. For example:

ACTIVITY

```
NICE ----------------------NORMAL ----------------------RUDE
_____           I have no money              _____

This soup is interesting     _____              _____

_____              _____             That's bullshit!
```

4.2 Collocation and predictability

In the previous chapter I referred several times to the crucial ability of prediction in language use. Indeed, much of what we call learning is the accumulation of predictive stores that allow us, on the basis of minimal clues in the input, to determine accurately what is going on, and predict with a reasonable degree of success what is going to happen next. As examples of such stores I mentioned stories, scripts, schemas, and frames (all these are so closely related that it is not possible to keep them neatly separate).

In addition to these cognitive storage systems, MOPS or

Memory Organizational Packages', as Roger Schank has called them (see Green, *Understanding Language: A Cognitive Approach* (1985)), the language we speak and hear is itself organized in such a way that it facilitates prediction. We can note this in intonation patterns, in the ways that syntax mirrors logic (the cause before the effect), chronology, space (from close to far, from left to right), and topic relatedness, and in the way language is embedded in social and cultural rituals which unfold in time-honoured ways.

A further way in which language sets up its own predictions is through the phenomenon of <u>collocation</u>, which can be defined as the habitual association of words or expressions with one another. The word habitual sounds a note of warning, and at the same time explains why we do not tend to find a great deal of attention paid to collocation in the average grammar book (though there are now some collocational dictionaries, e.g. Benson et al, 1986 and the Longman Language Activator, 1993): collocation is not governed by clear rules which can be articulated and explained, rather it just 'happens'. This quality of haphazardness, combined with its low instructional profile, makes collocation an extremely tricky aspect of language learning.

To show how collocation works, try the exercise below. This exercise tends to be quite easy for the native speaker of English, and very difficult for the non-native speaker, even the very advanced one. In this exercise, every adjective naturally (habitually) collocates with one of the nouns on the right. Although some combinations other than the ones suggested work as well (for example, professionally built, perfectly true), it should be possible, by gradual elimination, to match the pairs as suggested in the Key. The fact that this is possible shows that, in our writing and speaking, we orient towards collocatable items. In some cases collocations are so strong and conventionally joined that they turn into clichés, at which point the style-conscious user will begin avoiding them. This may be the case with *fatally flawed* (notice, by the way, that many collocations employ alliteration).

In addition to adjective–noun collocations, there are many other conventional combinations, such as partitive constructions:

a cup of coffee
a jar of peanut butter
a piece of chalk
a stick of gum

ACTIVITY

Match the adjective on the left to the corresponding noun on the right:

4e

fatally	*plain*
sincerely	*wooded*
undoubtedly	*obvious*
dazzlingly	*true*
impeccably	*flawed*
carefully	*furnished*
solidly	*beautiful*
densely	*designed*
tastefully	*yours*
professionally	*attired*
painfully	*crafted*
perfectly	*built*

(Author's data)

On a more folkloric note, the famous rhyming slang of London's cockney dialect, a two-stage code, can only work because it exploits collocation as well as rhyme:

4f

$\leftarrow---$ Stage 2: collocation	$\leftarrow---$ Stage 1: rhyme
titfer	tit-for-tat	(hat)
daisies	daisy roots	(boots)
loaf	loaf of bread	(head)
plates	plates of meat	(feet)
trouble	trouble and strife	(wife)

(Author's data)

The collocations illustrated here are only the tip of the iceberg as far as the <u>design for predictability</u> of language is concerned. Ease of prediction (as well as its opposite, creativity and invention) is designed into the very core of language and is manifested in many different ways. As an example, think of how many times politicians make 'three points' in their speeches, or use structures like: 'Something is THIS, so-and-so is THAT, such-and-such is THE OTHER!!!' (thunderous applause). Such public speaking techniques, including applause elicitation, have been analysed by Max Atkinson in his fascinating book *Our Masters' Voices*. Further, in scientific papers the author often gives several views or definitions of a topic, ending up with his or her own, which of course is the preferred one: 'some have said x, others have said y, but I say z.'

The predictability design which permeates language in many different ways, and which also hooks language, culture and mind together with multiple connections, is rarely made explicit in language courses, grammar books, or writing tutorials (note the predictable three-part structure I used here!). The reason is that such design features do not come to us through explanation and rule learning, but rather are acquired through exposure, feel and habit. They are imbibed gradually through rich and meaningful contact with, and participation in, language.

4.3 Metaphor

Experienced teachers often say that the mark of a good teacher is the ability to give examples, and to create analogies and metaphors. An important word used by the good teacher is the word 'like', not in the colloquial sense of 'That's, like, bitchin', dude!' but in the sense of 'A is like B', where A is something new or abstract, and B is something known or concrete.

Howard Gardner, in his book *The Unschooled Mind*, said that 'a skilled teacher is a person who can open a number of different windows on the same concept' (1991, page 246). On another occasion Gardner (known for his theory of multiple intelligences) commented, in a similar vein:

First of all, when you are trying to present new materials, you cannot expect them to be grasped immediately. (If they are, in fact, the understanding had probably been present all along.) One must approach the issues in many different ways over a significant period of time if there is to be any hope of assimilation. (*To Open Minds*, (1989) page 158–9).

Saying things in a different way is the essence of **metaphor**. Its interpretation, as well as its manufacture, is a creative endeavour, and the philosopher Donald Davidson has called metaphor 'the dreamwork of language' (*Enquiries into Truth and Interpretation*, 1984, page 245). The reasons for using metaphors are various. Apart from the purpose of making difficult concepts clear, as in the educational uses mentioned above, metaphor may serve an aesthetic function, since we may use it as a way to use language decoratively, expressively, or dramatically. Metaphor therefore attests to the creative as well as the pedagogical (or didactic) power of language, and in this sense it contrasts with the conventional, routinized, or predictive function we discussed in the previous section. A metaphor has the potential to surprise (although a great many have been embedded in the language for so long that we accept them as a matter of course), whereas a collocation merely confirms our predictions.

These two forces exemplified by metaphor and collocation are central to the dynamic structuring of language, and they create a constant tension with a resulting balance that may shift one way or another depending on person, situation or culture: creativity versus convention, new versus predictable, original versus routine (Yetta Goodman, in a plenary address at the TESOL convention in 1989, spoke of <u>convention</u> and <u>invention</u>, as two language forces in education, and this seems to be similar to what I have in mind).

The diagram on page 67 shows the two axes, with various language phenomena (genres, we might say) plotted in places where I think they fit (you may well want to shift them a bit, or add other types of language). The quadrants created by the picture refer to four language modes which we might recognize in everyday life.

I CREATIVE AND NON-CONVENTIONAL

This is the realm where metaphor is created, and where poetry is written. The further we move out along the diagonal, the more we drift into romanticism, mysticism ... until we don't know any longer 'what the heck is being said'. Other language uses in this corner might include puns, new jokes, novels and letters to friends.

II CREATIVE AND CONVENTIONAL

We note here that metaphor 'spills over' into this area, since it often becomes part of the language, rather than having to be created fresh every time. However, we can still appreciate the creative element. Metaphor overlaps with idiom, which is a fixed expression with a standard meaning. Idiom, in turn, overlaps with proverb, which in addition to being fixed and standard, has a didactic function, that is, it is a 'wise saying' that teaches a lesson. Grandma says: 'A stitch in time saves nine', and we know what she means. If we move further and further out along the diagonal here, we ultimately get to dogma, indoctrination, thought control and totalitarianism, passing lectures and sermons along the way.

III NON-CREATIVE AND NON-CONVENTIONAL

This is, in my view, a nasty corner to be in, since it focuses on survival in an unpredictable environment. From 'I want' and

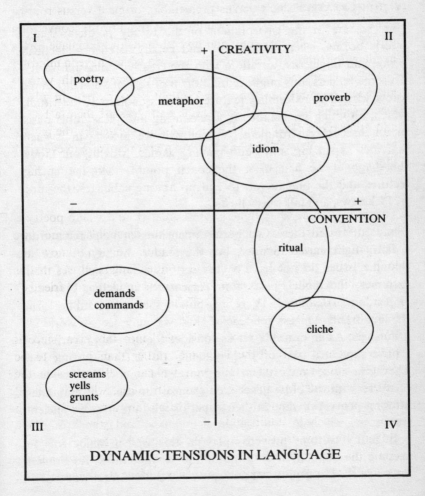

DYNAMIC TENSIONS IN LANGUAGE

'gimme' we descend, via grunts and yells, into an inferno of chaos and pandemonium, a jungle with predators but no defences. Extreme materialism, uncontrolled greed and raw fascism might dwell here (though, to succeed, fascism may have to team up with some of its like-minded colleagues from quadrant II).

IV NON-CREATIVE AND CONVENTIONAL

Here we are in the environment of the totally predictable and utterly boring, where idioms sink and petrify as clichés (a cliché being, you might say, an idiom with the creativity bled out of it). To some readers, this might remind them of school, though I don't know why. The redeeming feature of this quadrant is the ritual, which, although predictable, is a reassuring and pleasurable oasis in an insecure environment, especially if we include in it such activities as singing songs and playing games. Moving out along the diagonal we first meet the couch potato, then the boring lecturer and the bureaucrat, to end up among cabbages, the nine o'clock news, and talk-show hosts.

I have discussed these two basic dimensions of language use in a fairly lighthearted manner, but the reader should not assume that the issues do not have a very serious side as well. At their extremes, the model yields four caricatures of being: I mystic; II pendant; III animal; IV robot, but in their more subtle form the quadrants suggest tendencies that we may see at work all around us. As an example, let us consider the area of proverbs. As I have suggested, proverbs have a didactic, a teaching function. They give advice on prudent and moral behaviour. We associate proverbs with the older generation (hence, the cliché of grandmas uttering proverbs) who, in their superior wisdom, pass on ancient truths.

In many cultures proverbs play in this way a major role in keeping the population on a moral and sensible track. As Francis Bacon said, 'The genius, wit and spirit of a nation are discovered in its proverbs'. So, we can ask what it means when proverbs fall into disuse (along with, to make the situation more dramatic, the stories and fables of oral tradition). I remember when I first taught introductory linguistics to first-year university students in the US, and I happened to ask what a proverb was and if anyone could give an example. Not a single student in this large class could answer the question. After much prompting, and an example from me (A bird in the hand . . .), I think one or two examples came forth with great difficulty. 'But they are clichés,' offered one student, elaborating that the use of such language was not really very cool. One wonders where, in the absence of time-honoured linguistic formulas for good conduct, a new generation's morality, prudence and common sense might come from? Sources that have been suggested to me over the years include TV commercials, soap operas and perhaps even, at the moment of writing, that decidedly uncharming and self-proclaimedly moronic cartoon show *Beavis and Butthead*. In this show, everything is either 'cool', or else it 'sucks'.

An examination of patterns of language use may thus enable the critical language student to diagnose certain trends and propensities in a particular speech community (or discourse world). The way we use language undoubtedly reflects both individual and societal patterns of thought and changes of direction. Just as skin condition, changes in temperature and an analysis of body fluids helps the doctor diagnose the patient's state of health, a careful scrutiny of language use can tell a perceptive language user much about the health or sickness of society. This should of course not lead to the simplistic assumption that promoting changes in ways of speaking would automatically lead to the corresponding changes in society. The forces of political correctness, the Académie française and countless purists notwithstanding, things are unfortunately (or perhaps, fortunately!) never as simple as that.

4.4 Transparency revisited

In chapters 1 and 2 we noted that aspects of language can be relatively transparent or opaque. For example, a word like *bookcase* is more transparent than *wardrobe* since, for most people, 'ward' is not associated with keeping or putting away. In Spanish however, the equivalent word is *guardarropa*, literally 'keep-clothes'. Once we know that 'ward' is etymologically related to 'guard', the word *wardrobe* becomes somewhat more transparent. Transparent words (a technical term used sometimes is <u>morphologically motivated</u>) are easier to learn and remember than more opaque ones.

The notion of transparency is also useful when analysing metaphors, idioms and proverbs. *Look up to* and *look down on*, for example, are relatively transparent, since *up* and *down* have fairly predictable metaphorical (and idiomatic) uses in many cases:

4g

Up

Prices are going up

Things are looking up

He warmed up the soup

Down

I'm feeling down

I'm down to my last ten dollars

She downed three pints of McEwans

(Author's data)

Up means more expensive, more cheerful, hotter; *down* means cheaper, sadder, emptier, colder. Things are not always so clear-cut, however, to the consternation of language learners:

4h

Two blocks up	*Two blocks down*
I give up	*Don't back down*
Slow up!	*Slow down!*
Write up that essay	*Write down what I tell you*

(Author's data)

The same is true of other kinds of metaphorical expressions. Some are quite easy to figure out, others give very few clues to their intended interpretation. In addition, sometimes a speaker may want to innovate and make up a new metaphor, as when the radio announcer said: 'The stock market went south'. Try to guess the meaning of the following expressions or proverbs, translated literally from several languages:

ACTIVITY

4i

1. *The nail that sticks out must be hammered down (Japanese).*
2. *After the calf has drowned one closes the well (Dutch).*
3. *He doesn't need a grandmother (Spanish).*
4. *The apple does not fall far from the tree (Dutch).*
5. *He fell with his arse in the butter (Dutch).*
6. *To fear is not to sow because of the birds (Chinese).*

A *Like father, like son.*
B *Don't make waves, blend into the woodwork, be a team player.*
C *He hit gold, hit a home run, struck lucky.*
D *Nothing ventured, nothing gained.*
E *Don't close the stable door after the horse has bolted.*
F *He blows his own trumpet.*

(Author's data)

4j

Bomb Threat? No, He Meant His Bladder

FORT LAUDERDALE, Fla., Oct. 22 (AP) — An intoxicated German tourist's "bomb threat" aboard an airliner was actually a plea to go to the bathroom, a Federal district judge has ruled, nine months into the tourist's stay in prison.

The passenger told the German-speaking flight attendant that his bladder was about to explode, not the plane, a Federal judge says.

The passenger, Johann Peter Grzeganek, 23, who speaks little English, was freed on Wednesday but was back in custody on Thursday because his tourist visa had expired.

"It is a disgrace he's been in jail this long," the judge, Norman Roetger, told prosecutors. "Do you see anything that happened that couldn't have been remedied by letting this man go to the bathroom?"

Prosecutors agreed that Mr. Grzeganek, who had been held on charges of interfering with a flight crew and making a false bomb threat, should be freed from prison. But he was being held by immigration authorities for a flight to Germany.

The incident occurred in January on board an American Trans Air charter flight shortly after it took off from Fort Lauderdale for Hanover, Germany. Judge Roetger said Mr. Grzeganek used the German slang phrase for having to use the bathroom, which translated means, "Then the roof flies."

The flight attendant took that to mean a bomb was on board, and the pilot landed the plane at Hollywood-Fort Lauderdale International Airport.

(*New York Times*, 23 October 1993)

Sometimes proverbs or metaphorical expressions may be difficult to understand, or may be misunderstood. In the newspaper article on the left, you can see how such a misunderstanding landed a German tourist in some very deep trouble. Perhaps the Dutch proverb might have been useful for him: *When the wine is in the man, is the wisdom in the can*. The flight crew, on the other hand, should remember that *A little knowledge* (of German) *is a dangerous thing*, but at the time they were perhaps thinking *Better safe than sorry*. The overall story can perhaps best be summed up with *For want of a nail, the kingdom was lost*.

4.5 Pice of peep, piece of pipe, or pipe of peace?

From time to time people make interesting errors in their language use. Very often this involves switching parts of an expression around, or combining parts of two different expressions. Psycholinguists study such errors since they may give a glimpse of how language is organized in the brain. For example, if people say *pice of peep* or *piece of pipe*, instead of *pipe of peace*, this must mean that they had the second word in mind already before they uttered the first. Studies of so-called slips of the tongue suggests that language is produced not word by word, but in chunks of various kinds and lengths (collocations, idioms, phrases etc). At the moment of phonological production, certain sounds later in a unit can interfere with (for example, replace) sounds earlier in a unit. For this to be possible, a chunk of speech must be 'in mind' (Levelt, *Speaking* 1989, refers to this as 'lookahead') at the moment of producing the slip. Here are a few examples of slips of the tongue (they are also called spoonerisms, after a Revd Spooner of Oxford, who was in the habit of making such errors) that I have collected from radio, TV, or various conversations. See if you can explain how these slips might have come about.

ACTIVITY

4k

— *Tomorrow we'll have right lane – or rather light rain.*
— *. . . until the fasten turnbelt seat is signed off (I heard this on a plane; no one seemed to notice it).*
— *a sea communications – a key communications site].*
— *. . . if convected of – convicted of a felony.*
— *. . . bringing us up to bait – er . . . up to date rather, about the debate.*
(Author's data)

These errors are based on a phonological production problem. Another type of error is based on word choice: a particular word is intended, but another word, similar in spelling or pronunciation, is chosen. Or perhaps a similar-sounding familiar word is substituted for a less familiar one. These errors are often called malapropisms, after Mrs Malaprop, a character in Sheridan's play *The Rivals* (in recent years, a popular TV character, Archie Bunker, has produced his own brand of such errors, 'bunkerisms'). In the following list, which is the word the speaker intended?

ACTIVITY

4l

— *Let me divert for a moment here.*
— *The bustle of downtown Tokyo is testament to its commercial superiority . . .*
— *They are just trying to use us as an escape goat.*
— *As soon as there's a chink in the armoury, there's problems, you see, you gotta patch up the dyke.*

A final type of error I want to illustrate is one in which half of an expression is stuck together with half of another expression, creating a mixed form which we might call a griffin (or gryphon), after the mythological beast which was half eagle, half lion. Here are some examples. What are the two expressions that were mixed?

ACTIVITY

4m

— *I'm writing full stop.*
— *It clearly was a . . . default on our part.*
— *The economy is beginning to perk along just a little bit.*
(Author's data)

4.6 Oxymorons and other oddities

In various parts of this chapter we have spoken of such lexical phenomena as euphemism, metaphor and spoonerism. There are a number of other word processes which have specific names, and the quiz below allows you to test your knowledge of them — and to increase your esoteric vocabulary.

ACTIVITY

4n

1. *Lift your legs, and spirits* *(advertisement for footrest)*	A *Spoonerism*
2. *. . . . until the fasten turnbelt seat is signed off.* *(airline hostess)*	B *Oxymoron*
3. *Let me <u>divert</u> for a moment here.* *(President George Bush)*	C *Metaphor*
4. *. . . a certain amount of <u>controlled chaos</u>* *(News: riots in Cologne)*	D *Euphemism*

5. *A: Time for lunch! Where's the <u>roachcoach</u>?*
    B: Heheh – the good ol' <u>maggot wagon</u>.
       (workers at a construction site)
	E *Zeugma*

6. *Congress <u>piling up the pork</u>, critics say* *(Newspaper headline, about pork-barrel politics)*	F *Pun*
7. *. . . . creating <u>a context of plausible deniability</u>*	G *Dysphemism*
8. *He was <u>let go</u> (that is, fired)*	H *Malapropism*
9. *You can be <u>pre-approved in advance.</u>*	I *Gobbledygook*
10. *<u>Hair today</u>, spray tomorrow?* *(Dave Barry column)*	J *Tautology*

(Author's data)

In this chapter we have looked at some aspects of the meaning of words and expressions. I have taken a fairly low-key approach to the power of words, since I shall come back to such issues as prejudice and linguistic violence in chapter 7.

When we look in a dictionary or a language textbook we tend to get the impression that words have well-defined and precise meanings, that are evoked every time the word is used or heard. However, I hope it is clear now that this is not the case: connotations, metaphorical usage and predictions all mean that we often have to calculate the meaning of a particular word every time anew, in the context in which it is uttered, bearing in mind the speaker's supposed purpose. Of course, we also do a lot of routine interpreting, just sliding along a well-oiled groove of predictable interactions and meanings. But careful examination, even of the most casual conversation, reveals that we frequently pay close attention to the assessment, the weighing, the exact mix of ingredients, in the 'simmering pot of meanings' that words are. Meanings do not sit inside words like baked beans in a can, waiting for us to pour them out. We put meanings in words by using them in particular contexts (using context in its widest sense). In a sense then, we construct the meaning of words as we speak them and as we hear them, because there are many ways in which they accrue meanings from our context and our purposes. Sometimes those meanings may resemble what it says in the dictionary, but there is usually more around, behind and ahead of them.

Language is often called the mirror of society, or indeed of the individual ('you are as you speak'), but perhaps it is more accurate to say that it is just as much a <u>tool</u> with which we construct our world, the pencil with which we draw the picture of life.

PROJECT

Select an area of vocabulary or a context (for example, business, computer use, medicine, marketing, TV commercials; or idioms, proverbs, euphemisms, and so on) and conduct an analysis of the use of special words and expressions in that area. It is also interesting to compare a particular area of use across two languages. Write an illuminating and entertaining essay (about the size of a newspaper column) which reports your findings.

SUMMARY

- Words usually do not have one single meaning, but a range of meanings, depending on the context in which they are used, and the intentions and interpretations of speakers and listeners.
- In addition to denotative (literal) content, most words also have connotations, which may be positive or negative.
- Certain words often habitually occur together, that is, are collocated; this makes both production and interpretation easier, but it is very difficult to give any rules for collocation.
- Collocation can be said to be one of the conventional aspects of language. A major element in the creativity of language is metaphor, in which one word or expression replaces another.
- Slips of the tongue and other speech errors are often used by psycholinguists as clues to the way language is organized in the brain, and how speech is produced.

5   Correctness

In 1989 an article appeared in the New York *Times* which reported
a new scheme by the Schools Chancellor to improve the way New
Yorkers speak English. According to the article, Mayor Ed Koch
wholeheartedly endorsed the plan. The article, and the list of
'speech demons' identified by the Chancellor, is reproduced on
page 80. It raises some interesting questions:
— Why would certain people be 'offended' by the way others
  speak?
— What do you think are the chances of success of the purification
  effort?
— How can we tell good from bad speech habits?

Looking at the list of 'demons', you may perhaps find some that
you do not find 'offensive' at all, and others that you never knew
existed, except if you happen to be from New York. Unless you are
from the US, you may not know what's wrong with 'Can I leave
the room'. In order to drive out that particular demon you need to
know that generations of American children have been told that
'May I' is polite and proper, whereas 'Can I' is impolite and even
nonsensical, since, from this view, '*can*' is literally taken as expressing
ability, not permission.

You may observe further that some of the examples can identify
their speaker on regional (*you betcha*) or racial (*axe, he be sick*)
grounds. In other words, the linguistic items singled out for purification are much more likely to be heard in Harlem or the Bronx,
or from the mouths of recent arrivals from uncivilized places west
of the Hudson, than from those who dwell in high places along
Park Avenue, or among the green lawns of Scarsdale. This means

Purging 'What-Cha' and 'Ain't'

By NEIL A. LEWIS

Special to The New York Times

NEW YORK, Feb. 27 — New York City's Schools Chancellor, Richard R. Green, is beginning a campaign to purge New York of New Yorkese and other offending speech patterns.

In a memorandum to Mayor Edward I. Koch released today, Dr. Green identified 20 phrases or mispronunciations, some peculiar to New York, he is determined to eliminate from the speech of city students.

Listing 'Speech Demons'

The items supposed to be corrected include the cheery "whatcha doin?" ("what are you say'ng?," "students will be taught to say," to the hoary bane of English teachers, ain't. Malefactors being questioned should learn not to say: "I don't know nuttin about it." Instead, they should respond with a proper: "I don't know anything about it."

poster contest will be held to "focus on common errors in the oral use of language."

Dr. Green said he would convene in April "a working group of outstanding educators, including representatives of the university community, the New York Public Libraries and Central Office experts" to develop a long-term plan, Dr. Green wrote.

Plan Called 'Superb'

In releasing the Chancellor's program today, Mr. Koch pronounced it "superb."

Included on the list are some of the speech patterns the Mayor singled out in a letter to Dr. Green as particularly offensive — saying "axe" for "ask," for example, and the misuse of the verb "to be" as in "He be sick."

Among the 20 problems cited by the Chancellor is the mispronunciation of the word "library" as "liberry," a mistake the Mayor has acknowledged he occasionally makes himself.

Demons Possessing Student Tongues

May I *axe* a question?	May I ask a question?
Hang the *pitcher* on the wall.	Hang the picture on the wall.
He's *goin'* home.	He's going home.
He *be* sick.	He is sick.
I *ain't* got none.	I don't have any.
Can I leave the room?	May I leave the room?
I was *like* tired, *you know?*	I was tired.
Where is the ball *at?*	Where is the ball?
What-cha doin'?	What are you doing?
I'll *meetcha* at the *cau-nuh.*	I'll meet you at the corner.
What do *youse* want?	What do you want?
Let's go to *da* center.	Let's go to the center.
I *brang* my date along.	I brought my date along.
The books *is* in the *liberry.*	The books are in the library.
Yup, you betcha!	Yes, you're right.
Pacifically, . . .	Specifically, . . .
I don't know *nuttin* about it.	I don't know anything about it.
I'm *not* the *only* one.	I'm not the only one.
We was *on'y foolin' 'round.*	We were only fooling around.
So, I says to him . . .	So, I said to him . . .

(New York Times, 27 February 1989)

that speaking well is associated with certain groups of people, and speaking badly with others. It is no doubt the case that at times race, ethnicity, social class, or geographical origin, play a role in judgements of proper speech. In addition to (or on top of) such factors, the general argument in favour of good speech is that it is a mark of being well-educated. Since being well-educated is universally valued good, this last argument can always be used to promote some form of standard language, without the danger of being accused of racism, prejudice, or bigotry. However, this argument does not rule out that, underneath the rational surface, certain biased attitudes or prejudices may actually be stoking the pot of purism from the unseen depths of a person's psyche.

Linguistic purism, or in general the promotion of a standard language, the desire for a pure and proper language unspoiled by barbarisms, foreign imports, grammatical aberrations and other abominations, is not confined to prominent officials in New York. There is no doubt that every reader, from whatever corner of the globe, can find examples of it in his or her own environment, particularly of course in the schools. From the Dutch (in spite of their reputation of being very tolerant) and their *Algemeen Beschaafd Nederlands* (that is, Generalized Civilized Dutch, thus equating 'speaking the standard language' with 'being civilized'), to the French and their Académie Française, to the school in Greece where only British English (Received Pronunciation, of course) is taught and American English is shunned, value judgements on one way of speaking versus another, one dialect versus another, or one accent versus another, are commonplace.

When we study language, whether our own or a subsequent one, the question of correctness often looms large, magnified by the pedagogical efforts of all parties involved. Students, no doubt conditioned by years of grammar-grinding activities, and teachers, who engage in such grinding because it seems to be required by tradition, see only one question whenever they are confronted with a new piece of language: is this correct, or is it incorrect? They are so blinded by correctness that true appreciation of language and the creative joy of discovery are blocked from view.

The ogre of correctness is largely responsible for the dullness that characterizes most language study, whether in grammar lessons, foreign language classes, or university classes in linguistics. It even invades, very often, the study of literature. It is as if we studied Van Gogh's paintings by boiling them in a large vat of vinegar, separating the colours by spectroscopy, and hanging the soggy canvases out to dry. As a result of our obsession with correctness there seems to be only one way to teach language: badly.

Language awareness must include a conscious effort to put correctness in its proper place: a social phenomenon, on a par with dress codes and table manners, but not an integral part of the study of language. In this chapter we will make a small contribution to this effort.

5.1 Test your grammatical tolerance

A few years ago I taught a beginners grammar class to a group of Asian, mostly Japanese, students. I soon found out that these adolescents actually had an amazing knowledge of English grammar, far in excess of most well-educated native speakers. They had no trouble at all identifying adverbs of frequency, causative constructions and non-restrictive relative clauses. However, if you asked them to write down an informally spoken utterance like 'Can I have some more milk, please,' they were unable to do so, however many times it was played back to them.

In an effort to get them used to everyday casual English I asked them to bring a small index card to class every time, on which they had written (no matter the spelling) something they had heard out on the streets or in the cafeteria. As a result of moving out of the grammar book (where everything is always correct) and into the real world (where all sorts of things can be heard, all the time), one of the most frequent questions in the class became: 'Teacher, is X correct?' and I found myself frequently having to answer, 'In that particular context, it sounds all right,' or, 'Not according to the grammar book, but people say it all the time,' and so on. Most of the time, my wishy-washy answer did not satisfy the students, who must have thought they had either a nincompoop or a dangerous anarchist for a teacher.

Out of sheer desperation I finally devised a 'grammar stick' (by analogy to yardstick) which allowed me to indicate grammatical judgements which were not either black or white, but indicated shades of acceptability in context. This grammar stick has turned out a most useful device in the quest of weaning students away from their correct–incorrect mindset. Because variation according to formality and politeness is often an issue in judgements of 'correctness', I eventually also added a crossbar roughly corresponding to levels of formality (taken from Martin Joos's *Five Clocks*). In this form it is reproduced below as text **5b**.

The grammar stick depicted here aspires neither to scientific accuracy nor to grammatical perfection, but its very imprecision symbolizes the makeshift nature of our judgements. It clearly does not deal very well with context (having merely two measures explicitly referring to this: 7 and 4, and its four spaces may insufficiently distinguish between grammar and good taste:

I   informal to intimate
II   formal to distant
III   terribly rude
IV   awkwardly offish

For all its imperfection, such an evaluation device (or an improved version devised by ingenious readers), when put up on the classroom wall as a poster, allows a teacher to point to a particular space or number whenever the question 'correct or incorrect?' comes up. If nothing else, this will wean students away from an overly black-and-white view of correctness and grammaticalness.

5b
GRAMMAR STICK DE LUXE

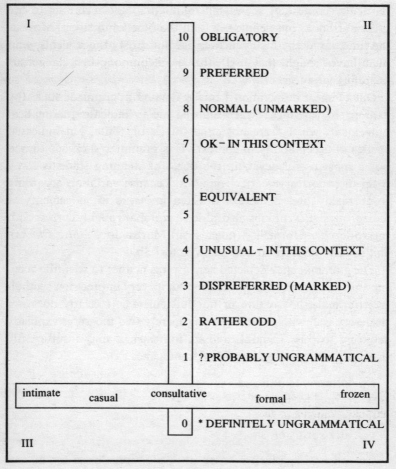

10	OBLIGATORY
9	PREFERRED
8	NORMAL (UNMARKED)
7	OK – IN THIS CONTEXT
6	
	EQUIVALENT
5	
4	UNUSUAL – IN THIS CONTEXT
3	DISPREFERRED (MARKED)
2	RATHER ODD
1	? PROBABLY UNGRAMMATICAL

intimate   casual   consultative   formal   frozen

0	* DEFINITELY UNGRAMMATICAL

(Author's data)

For a practical demonstration, I would like the reader to complete the grammatical tolerance test on page 86. Ignoring, for this particular exercise, the crossbar, and imagining, for the sake of the exercise, a convenient context when necessary, please evaluate the twenty sentences on the scale from 0–10 suggested by the grammar stick. If you have a chance to compare with someone else, it might also be interesting to write down and then compare any correction you think might be in order. Finally, you can obtain your very own GTQ by doing the simple calculation suggested.

At the end, and after the revelation that all these sentences and utterances were produced by native speakers of English, I hope that you have a somewhat more graduated and a 'fuzzier' notion of what 'speaking correctly' might mean. In some cases you may have found a sentence incomprehensible, for example, in 11, you probably can't understand what *ollying all kinds of high* might mean, unless you live in California and you (or your kids) are into skateboarding: *ollying* means jumping so that all four wheels of the board are off the ground, and *all kinds of* means very. Or you may not know what, in 14, *neneks* are, and what they do when they *mengalay*, unless you have lived in Malaysia, and know that *nenek* means older woman, and *mengalay* is a kind of dance.

Listening to the language around you, you can hear all sorts of things. The one thing you do not hear are sentences of the type that used to be in grammar books: 'My nose is in the middle of my face'; 'Are you a girl? No, I am a boy'. Although grammar books have got a lot better in recent years, they still only contain language that, like dried flowers, has been cut and pressed between the pages. Language awareness does not mean sticking your nose into a grammar book or textbook in a more intense manner, rather, it means looking up and around, and pricking up your ears to hear and appreciate the language around you.

ACTIVITY

GRAMMATICAL TOLERANCE TEST

5c

* IS:	SHOULD(?)BE:
1. *He <u>dove</u> into the icy water.*	
2. *Is your house <u>rugged</u>? (/rʌgd/)*	
3. *These clothes need <u>washed</u>.*	
4. *There's a big meeting <u>ongoing</u> right now.*	
5. *The government <u>have</u> broken all <u>their</u> promises.*	
6. *OK, let's go in <u>already</u>.*	
7. *Hey, Valerie, you should've <u>came</u>.*	
8. *It's ten minutes <u>in front of</u> eight o'clock.*	
9. *It's getting hard to make ends meet <u>anymore</u>.*	
10. *Do you have <u>a</u> scissors?*	/
11. *Josh's brother can <u>olly all kinds of high</u>.*	
12. *Where's the library <u>at</u>?*	
13. *Could you <u>open</u> the television please? I want to watch the <u>news</u>.*	
14. *The sporting <u>neneks</u> sang and 'mengalaid' through the <u>night</u>.*	
15. *Are you <u>first</u> having lunch? (= this late?)*	
16. *This is strictly between you and <u>I</u>.*	
17. *We're <u>the busiest</u> this fall <u>than</u> ever before.*	
18. *An orderly evacuation is currently <u>undergoing</u>.*	
19. *<u>Also too</u>, on the back table, there are several <u>brochures</u> and application forms.*	
20. *As soon as there's a <u>chink in the armoury</u>, there's problems, you see, you gotta patch up the <u>dyke</u>.*	

* use the vertical scale on the grammar stick. Add all points and divide by 20 to obtain your GTQ.
(© 1993, Leo van Lier)

5.2 Spoken and written language

In most people's minds, written language has somehow more importance and authority than spoken language. 'It's true!' the saying goes, 'Because I read it in the newspaper.' Although most readers are probably not so naïve as to assume that everything that is printed must be true, it is no exaggeration to state that, over the centuries or millennia since the invention of writing, and especially since the invention of printing, the written word has assumed a position of dominance in our conscious dealings with language.

Whenever spoken and written language are compared, this is done by telling what the spoken language does not have, as compared to the written language. As a result, the spoken language is seen as less structured, less neat and tidy, less sophisticated and complex, and so on. Speech, in contrast to writing, is full of false starts, half-finished sentences, hesitations, uhms and ahs and other blemishes. As Michael Halliday puts it, 'there is a tradition of regarding spoken language as formless and featureless,' (*Spoken and Written Language* (1989), page 76). In fact, one of the most prominent theories of syntax of the last three decades, Chomsky's generative syntax, is based entirely on the analysis of written sentences, regarding spoken language simply as <u>performance</u>, affected by 'memory limitations, distractions, shifts of attention and interest and errors,' (Chomsky *Aspects of a Theory of Syntax* (1965), page 3).

In spite of this tradition I take the view that the spoken language is basic and primary (after all, languages were around for hundreds of thousands of years before writing was invented), and that writing was originally based on speech. This is not to deny, of course, the tremendous achievements of literature, or the fact that writing has a structure in its own right, but merely to argue that speech and writing must be examined separately, each on its own terms, and not one in terms of the other.

Spoken language is every bit as complex and intricate as written language, but it is so in very different ways. For example, as Halliday shows, speech is lexically sparse but grammatically complex, and writing is lexically dense but grammatically simple. This means that more words are crowded together in a piece of writing, but that spoken language has more intricate and denser grammatical patterns, often collaboratively produced by different speakers. Here are some of the basic differences, partly adapted from Halliday, 1989:

5d

Spoken	Written
auditory	*visual*
temporary; immediate reception	*permanent; delayed reception*
prosody (intonation, stress, rhythm)	*punctuation*
immediate feedback	*delayed or no feedback*
a variety of attention and boundary signals (including kinesic ones)	*attention, boundaries, pointers, etc, limited to verbal devices*
planning and editing limited by channel	*unlimited planning, editing, revision*
lexically sparse	*lexically dense*
grammatically dense	*grammatically simple*

(adapted from Halliday 1989)

It should be clear from the table that speech and writing have their own characteristics, and are appropriate for different purposes and situations.

One particular type of spoken language, conversation, is often singled out by sociologists (though not by linguists, as I indicated above) as having particular interest as an object of analysis (see also Ch. 3). Berger and Luckmann, for example, in their influential book *The Social Construction of Reality* (1966), argue that conversation is the most important means by which people maintain their real sense of reality. This is not done by explicitly discussing the nature of the world, but rather 'it takes place against the background of a world that is silently taken for granted' (page 172).

Conversation, by its very casualness, reassures us that the world is still there, and that we are still in it in our usual and proper place. At the same time, however, as I mentioned in chapter 3, within the apparent simplicity of conversation we do an enormous amount of work in presenting ourselves to others and sizing one another up. In that sense, conversation is of major importance to the way in which we construct our social world. It requires, in the words of Pierre Bourdieu,

unceasing vigilance . . . to manage this interlocking of prepared gestures and words; the attention to every sign . . . is indispensable, in the use of the most ritual pleasantries, in order to be carried along by the game without getting carried away by the game beyond the game, as happens when simulated combat gets the better of the combatants (*The Logic of Practice* (1990), pages 80–81).

Bourdieu also makes the astute observation that conversation includes the art of deliberately producing

ambiguous conduct that can be disowned at the slightest sign of withdrawal or refusal, and to maintain uncertainty about intentions that always hesitate between recklessness and distance, eagerness and indifference (ibid., page 81).

The reader might like to go back to the little conversation quoted on page 45, and examine it again in the light of Bourdieu's comments.

To summarize, spoken language is very different from written language on a number of dimensions, and has an importance that goes to the very centre of our existence. It has traditionally been much less studied than written language, and for that very reason we need to become aware of its various roles in our life.

5.2.1   A norsy zedandle

In language classes teachers often speak in a slow and careful manner, anxious to be understood by all students, and to give a perfect example of how the language is to be pronounced. Slurring words and swallowing every other syllable (notice how every language, except our very own, seems to be pronounced in such sloppy ways as to be all but unintelligible to non-natives), while it may be second nature in other circumstances, will just not do in the classroom. As a result of such super-careful speech or teacherese, many students hardly ever hear the language spoken at its normal speed, so that, when they finally find themselves in a foreign setting, they are totally helpless in spite of all their years of diligent study and their high marks in exams.

In order to bring this point home, I once recorded a native speaker saying, casually and informally:

Why don't you let me read it first.

I played this utterance back to a group of non-native teachers of English with the request to write it down. None of them could, not even after many replays. However, I had also recorded the same sentence as read, slowly and carefully, by a Japanese graduate student. When I played that second version, all confused faces immediately lit up. Understanding casual spoken language is thus a skill that does not come automatically with language study. Its interpretation requires a lot of practice in hearing the real thing.

For practice, try and find out what the following text means. It is
from an advertisement for a restaurant in Minneapolis, and illustrates what in Minnesota is known as 'range talk'.

5e

> # DJEETCHET?
> # NOJU?
> # SQUEET.
> # K.

(Author's data)

Next I turn to the rather peculiar heading of this section, which
may have been puzzling you. When discussing spoken language,
and dialects in particular (see the next section), I write this on the
board

A NORSY ZEDANDLE

inviting students to guess what it might mean, and sounding the
strange words out. In most cases, nobody can guess what the
words might mean. I then play Marriott Edgar's poem *The Lion
and Albert*, read in a Lancashire accent by Stanley Holloway,
asking students to listen out for the words in question. It turns out
that my mystery words refer to a phrase in the following verse:

> A grand little lad was young Albert
> All dressed in his best, quite a swell
> With a stick with **a horse's head handle**
> The finest that Woolworth's could sell.

The explanation for this change in the sound shape of the words is that in the Lancashire dialect the sound *h* is not pronounced. This brings about a change from *a* to *an*, changing *a horse* to *anorse*. The possessive *s*, pronounced as *z*, is linked to the vowel in *'ead*, producing *zed*, and finally the *d* of *zed* is linked to the *a* in *'andle*, producing *dandle*, and in this way we end up with *anorsyzedandle*.

Not a very consequential exercise for native speakers, perhaps, but it brings home the problem that foreign students (and to some extent all children: some readers may be familiar with the famous mishearing of 'Gladly the cross I'd bear' as 'Gladly, the cross-eyed bear') face when they have to segment the speech stream into words that make sense. We should not underestimate this task in any language, and the message for teachers and students alike is to listen to a lot of casual speech to get a feeling for the absorption patterns (or patterns of assimilation) in a language, and to play around with words and sounds so that these patterns become familiar. It should be noted that this is a complex affair which cannot be accomplished overnight, but will most likely take years.

5.3 Dialects

Dialects are recognizable varieties of a particular language. The line between dialect and language cannot be clearly drawn. It is often jokingly said that a language is a dialect with an army and a navy, since there seems to be no linguistic way to make the distinction. For example, there are many dialects in Chinese that are mutually unintelligible, and speakers of the dialects can only communicate through the writing system that they share. In fact, to communicate something they may draw a character in their hand with their finger, and this is generally recognizable. Similarly, in the long-drawn-out area where Quechua is spoken in the Andes, which once was the Inca empire, there are a variety of dialects which are all intelligible when they are adjacent or fairly close, but the further apart the dialects are geographically, the less intelligible they become to one another. By contrast, two languages like Danish and Swedish are by and large mutually intelligible, and so are Czech and Slovak.

Be that as it may, one should not offend a Dutch speaker by saying that he speaks a dialect of German (this has happened to me on occasion), or a Catalan that she speaks a dialect of Spanish. A similar insult, though one that often goes unnoticed, is made when it is said that Indians (Native Americans) speak their 'native dialect', or that hundreds of dialects are spoken in India. In both cases, the appropriate word should of course be language, not dialect.

Dialects are most often thought of as geographically determined, that is, different regions have different dialects. Thus, in the US, there are such varieties as Boston (and more generally, New England), Texan (more generally, Southern), New York (to the dismay, as we saw above, of the former Mayor). In most cases these are fairly big areas (especially in the case of Texas, of course), but in other parts of the world dialect patterns may be different. In the part of the Netherlands where I was born, Limburg, every village, however small, has its own recognizable dialect, so that the native can tell instantaneously where someone comes from, not unlike the legendary capabilities of Professor Higgins in Shaw's *Pygmalion*, who could track people down to the very street where they were born. To give you an example from my own background, within a radius of 20 kilometres from my home town, the word for *cold* can have at least the following pronunciations (it's /kɔwt/ in standard Dutch):

kɑ:w   kə:t   kɔ:t   kɑlt

Dialects are not exclusively based on regional differences, however. Other variables include age, social class, race and education. For example, in California, young people now like to preface direct reported speech with the expressions *X's all*, and *Y's (like)*), and *Z goes*. Here is an example from a newspaper interview:

5f

And she's all, 'Well, you're Filipino.'
I go, 'Yeah, I know I'm Filipino'.
She's all, 'I don't think you would feel comfortable –,
I go, 'How could you tell me how I'm going to feel?'

(San Jose *Mercury News*, 19 September 1993)

To test your dialect powers, I would like to end this section with a quiz on lexical dialect differences between British and American English. Match every item on the left with the corresponding one on the right.

ACTIVITY

TRIVIAL DIALECTOLOGY

5g

British	*American*
1. *spanner*	A. *RV*
2. *saloon*	B. *turnout*
3. *terrace*	C. *station wagon*
4. *juggernaut*	D. *wrench*
5. *guv'nor*	E. *town house*
6. *caravan*	F. *pooped*
7. *layby (n)*	G. *big rig*
8. *knackered*	H. *sedan*
9. *silencer*	I. *honcho*
10. *estate*	J. *muffler*

(Author's data)

In this chapter we have taken aim at the notion of correctness. I have suggested that, by and large, we have let the question of correct language overshadow other issues which are much more important for an understanding of language. Further, the question, 'Correct or incorrect?' masks the fact that language using is a living process that we need to appreciate and learn to understand better, not merely judge by a list of rules printed in a grammar book. That same question also ignores the essential diversity that exists in language use: regional differences, age differences and differences according to ethnic group, age, profession, and so on. It is hard to see such diversity as a blemish on language, since to argue so would be like saying that radio stations should only play one kind of music, say, songs by Frank Sinatra, and nothing else. It is often said that diversity is the spice of life but, in language, diversity serves a range of practical functions as well. It allows people to feel part of a group, giving a sense of belonging, and it also allows for more efficient and precise expression of concerns, activities, and objects in specific contexts. In some cases, a language variety can become a collective art form in which members of a group can show their verbal dexterity by creating new forms of expression (in many southern Dutch, Flemish and German villages, for example, carnival is a time when dialect use is celebrated through songs, comedy, poetry, story telling, and so on).

As students of language awareness we have to focus on spoken language in its own right (rather than 'through the eyes of' writing), we have to look behind issues of correctness to the dynamics of language use and diversity, and we have to appreciate rather than fear diversity. Bringing these principles and attitudes to school (as teachers, parents and students) would go a long way towards pulling language out of the dreary doldrums into which it has drifted over the years. In the next chapter we will take a closer look at language in education.

PROJECT

The issue of correctness can be addressed from different angles:

— Every language has its varieties and dialects, and various opinions and attitudes about them. At the same time, most countries have some form of standard or official dialect, whether overtly or not, and readers from different countries might survey the situation in their country, or a particular aspect of dialect or standard use. For instance, when I went to school in the Netherlands, I was not allowed to speak dialect in the classroom: it had to be General Civilized Dutch (ABN – or *Algemeen Beschaafd Nederlands*). Is this the same in other countries? What variety are news readers supposed to speak? In the US it is some kind of midwest (so-called 'neutral') accent, sometimes called American Network English.

— Another project is to find out what teachers mean by 'correct language', and how they go about 'enforcing' it in their classrooms.

— Finally, it is interesting to collect, from the newspaper, radio and TV, articles and comments that address correctness in one form or another. Quite regularly, for example, one can find letters to advice columns ('Dear Abbey,' etc) asking about (or complaining about) some aspect of linguistic etiquette. Many newspapers also carry special language columns.

SUMMARY

- Opinions on correct or standard language are often mixed up with particular attitudes towards certain groups of people.
- An excessive emphasis in schools on correctness can turn language teaching into an uninteresting and demotivating enterprise.
- Spoken and written language are different in a number of ways, and have to be studied in their own right.

- Students of language need frequent and consistent practice in understanding casual spoken language, which differs from slow, formal speech in a number of systematic ways, for example, because of characteristic absorption patterns.
- Dialects often have significant value for the groups who speak them, and this means that they do not readily disappear, even where a standard language is dominant through the media and education.

6 Language in education

In chapter 1, I gave a brief overview of developments in language education in recent years. I suggested that the overall issue of language in education has in recent decades been neglected, or at least, dealt with in a piecemeal and rather haphazard fashion. It seems that curricula have swung like a pendulum from grammar grind to neglect and so on, back and forth. Language awareness, which I would like to see closely tied to educational linguistics (a discipline which does not exist in the way that, for example, educational psychology does, though perhaps it should; see van Lier 1994; see also Spolsky 1978, Stubbs 1986), has as one of its most crucial tasks to examine language in education as a goal (language arts, literacy, other languages) and as a vehicle (learning through lecturing, through conversation, through reading, through critical thinking, and so on).

People use language to express themselves, to relate to others and to get things done. It is so central a part of our lives that it is of the utmost importance to control it well, to grow it as strong and rich as possible, and to keep working at those tasks in a spirit of lifelong language learning. Second language learning fits into such a goal, since, as is often said, we learn much about our own language when we are learning another. Furthermore, another language opens up our world of ideas, broadens it, makes it flexible and frees it from the straitjacket of one single mode of thinking and expression. As Schopenhauer said, long ago:

In learning any foreign language, you form new concepts, you discover relationships you didn't realize before, innumerable nuances, similarities, differences enter your mind; you get a rounded view of everything. Which means that you think differently in every language, that learning a language modifies and colors your thinking, corrects and improves your views, and increases your thinking skill, since it will more and more detach your ideas from your words. (quoted in Flesch, *The Art of Clear Thinking* (1951), page 49).

But it is not only foreign language learning, nor only native language arts, that need to come under the scrutiny of language awareness. Language is central to all subject matters taught in schools, whether it be art, science, mathematics, or social studies. Not only is information conveyed through the medium of language (by lecturing, demonstrating, modelling, discussing, explaining, exemplifying and so on), an equally if not more important aspect is the message of expectations, encouragement, respect and responsibility that is carried in language use.

Finally, schools and school personnel use language to communicate with one another, thus establishing the school's world of discourse, and to communicate with parents and other entities in the community, thus confirming the place of the school in the

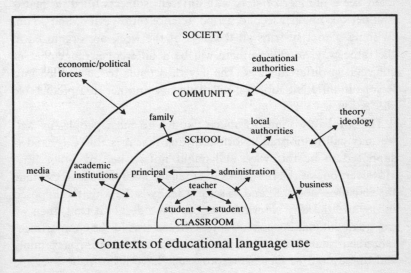

Contexts of educational language use

world, and negotiating the relations of the school with and within its community.

All these uses of language in education speak clearly to the usefulness of a systematic and careful study of language awareness in educational settings. There is much work that has been done in different aspects of educational language use, but an overall vision, a theory of language use in education, does not exist. It would be my hope, and my guess, that such a theory could bring many improvements to teaching and learning, because almost everything that gets done in schools is done through language. If we want to play music, we need to know our instrument well. If we want to educate, we need to know our language inside out, and play it with virtuosity and authenticity.

6.1 Language across the curriculum

If we look at a curriculum chart in a principal's office, we will most likely see a number of slots with different subjects filled in: maths first period, English second period, science third period, and so on. In some school systems all the days of the week are organized in the same way, in others there will be a different arrangement of subjects on different days. The day thus tends to be divided into lessons in different subjects, following one another in a predictable succession.

This probably sounds familiar enough to most people, in fact, we may call it 'normal'. Normal means that it is this way, and is supposed to be this way, and ought not to be any other way. However, one of the first tasks of language awareness is to examine the so-called 'normal', and to see if it really is the way it's supposed to be, and the way we want it to be. If we decide it isn't, then we can go about making some changes. In the case of the compartmentalized curriculum described above, such an examination is certainly warranted, and in fact many proposals have been made over the years to change to a different structure, whether it be called an open school, an integrated curriculum, a thematic approach, or systemic reform.

One of the things that will happen when we look for meaningful change is a return to focusing on broad overall goals, the basic philosophy or vision, the guiding principles in short, of the school. In a compartmentalized, pigeon-holed curriculum, points of detail, fragmentary concerns and day-to-day, subject-by-subject, department-by-department problem solving tend to take over. Let us look at some examples of language issues in schools that illustrate the need for a language across the curriculum perspective.

Just recently I have spent quite some time (as a parent representative) with a group of school personnel, including a principal, teachers and administrative staff, discussing curricular issues, the new technology that keeps bombarding us from all sides and the general direction of the school. What engaged our energies most, in these discussions, was the tentative formulation of a vision statement that would capture the overall spirit and aspirations of the school. This means pouring into a common language mould many highly complex and only partially articulated ideas and notions, in such a way that the result is both clear and pleasing, as well as acceptable and inspirational, to all the parties concerned, all the 'stakeholders', as the current term goes. A particular concern of the principal was that this vision statement should not be seen as a product to be accepted or rejected, but as a process which would invite continuous involvement and evolution through discussion and participation. Looking at language as a process, and using language to describe a process, are extremely difficult tasks. It is like drawing a picture of something that moves continually: it is hard to draw, and it is even harder to draw the movement itself.

The second example addresses teacher–parent–student interaction, and I would like to quote a part of an interaction I wrote down at an open-house night in an elementary school.

101

6a

Teacher (to boy):	*Does your mother have any questions?*
Child (to mother):	*Dice la profesora si tienes alguna pregunta.*
	(the teacher asks if you have any questions)
Mother (to teacher):	*Aah . . . pos, como se porta mi hijo?*
	(aah . . . well, how does my son behave?)
Child (to mother):	*How do I behave?*
Teacher (to mother):	*Oh, he behaves very good.*
Child (to mother):	*Dice que me porto muy bien. (she says that I behave very well)*

(Author's data)

The importance of parental involvement in education, and of school–home communication, hardly needs stressing. How the school–home dialogue is actually carried, however, is an extremely important topic for research, and an area of language awareness of foremost concern to teachers, since they are the main 'authorities' in that dialogue, and therefore set the tone in most situations. In the above example, an extra dimension is added to the already difficult area of teacher–parent interaction: the fact that teacher and mother do not share a common language. Notice how the child is used as a linguistic go-between, conveying information about himself from one person to another. Even more important, however, is the nature of that information. Basically, nothing of substance is said, beyond a ritual affirmation of 'good behaviour'. Now it is of course possible that neither teacher nor parent want to go beyond the ritualistic 'good behaviour' statement. That we shall never know, but the crucial point to be made is that the way the interaction is set up practically forces both parties to limit themselves to trivialities, rather than to engage in meaningful pedagogical discussion.

How can language awareness help in such situations? First, I suggest, by seeing and hearing examples such as this. Second, by thinking about them and discussing them with colleagues. Third, by becoming more aware of our own practices in similar situations.

Fourth, by finding imaginative ways to deal with a problem. Christopher Candlin used to say, in graduate seminars, that a constraint, when turned around, often becomes a resource. In this case, the constraint (linguistic incommunication) can become the resource to use the obvious interpreter's skills of the boy as a learning opportunity, and a boost to respect and self-respect. Instead of being a sort of metaphorical phone line linking two adults, the bilingual expertise of the child can be exploited to bring about meaningful educational dialogue. In such a scenario (think of portfolios, posters, presentations, simultaneous interpreting), everybody wins several times around, whereas in the above example, I think, everybody lost dismally.

For a third example, let's move into the actual classroom. The following extract is from an **ESL** class I taught some time ago, and involves making a list of countable/uncountable nouns on the blackboard:

6b

1 *A: Countable and uncountable, very good. Nouns. All of them are nouns . . . Okay. We need one person to help. Uh, Y? Can you help me? You come right here . . . you'll be the writer . . . the chief writer. Please . . . think of some things that go on each side . . . countable and uncountable nouns . . . that you remember . . . K, can you give us an example?*

2 *K: Uh, countable . . . tea . . .*

3 *A: Okay, tea, good. (to Y:) Write it down.*

4 *B: Wine.*

5 *A: What did you say? I'm sorry, I didn't hear you.*

6 *B: Wine.*

7 *A: Wine. Okay. Some more things. R, can you think of one? On this side maybe?*

8 *R: Students.*

9 *A: Students. Very good. Okay . . .*

(Author's data)

Here we see several people interacting with one another in a classroom. One of these is the teacher, and I don't suppose you will have much trouble deciding who that is. As a little awareness-raising activity, please compare this extract with the short conversation quoted on page 45. Below, list some of the differences you can see. Some of the cells are filled in to get you started.

quoted on page 45

ACTIVITY

6c

	Classroom extract	*Conversation*
turn taking	*controlled by teacher*	
nomination	*teacher nominates next speaker*	
questions		*both (all) parties*
answers		*both (all) parties*
evaluation		*answers / statements are not routinely evaluated*
elicitation		
predictable	*rather predictable in terms of who speaks about what, and when*	
other?		

(Author's data)

As you can appreciate, there are a number of striking differences between the classroom extract and the conversation. The exact ramifications of this observation will be discussed in more detail in another section below.

As the above discussion shows, language is intimately intertwined with all aspects of education, the entire curriculum, up and down and across the school, and in its connections with the society in which it is situated. Language awareness in education has as its aim to examine this language systematically, and then to use our powers of language use to make the changes that we deem necessary. To put the argument in another way, we gain control over language by understanding it, and in that understanding we can use language to control our environment rather than have it slip out of control.

6.2 The role of language in teacher education

Among teachers of English in general and those who write on usage in particular, even a small degree of formal linguistic training is still the exception rather than the rule. (D. Baron *Grammar and Good Taste* (1982), New Haven: Yale University Press, page 227).

According to the French sociologist Pierre Bourdieu, the school is an institution in which correct ('legitimate') language is perforce transmitted to students. In Bourdieu's view, teachers get their notion of correct language from the grammarians who are in charge of 'fixing and codifying' language, and they then proceed to impose this correct language on the students 'through innumerable acts of correction'. You may wish to reflect on this or discuss it with colleagues, thinking of examples from your experience that either confirm or contradict this rather stark view of the role of language in education:

. . . legitimate language is a semi-artificial language which has to be sustained by a permanent effort of correction, a task which falls both to institutions specially designed for this purpose and to individual speakers. Through its grammarians, who fix and codify legitimate usage, and its teachers who impose and inculcate it through innumerable acts of correction, the educational system tends, in this area as elsewhere, to produce the need for its own services and its own products, i.e. the labour and instruments of correction. P. Bourdieu, *Language and Symbolic Power* (1991), Cambridge, MA: Harvard University Press, pages 60–61.

Now let's compare the quote from Bourdieu with the one from Dennis Baron that opens this section. Baron says that very few teachers have any degree of proper ('formal') linguistic training to speak of. Shelving for the moment the issue of what formal linguistic training is or ought to be, we have here a situation in which teachers force upon their students a certain codified, legitimate language, but it is a type of language which they themselves are not experts in, rather they take its characteristics on authority from the grammarians (whoever and wherever they may be). These grammarians, however, have. not dissected and analysed language from a pedagogical perspective, but rather from a purely linguistic one. There may thus be a gap between linguistic theory and language education which results in inadequate teaching practices.

Once again, you need to decide for yourself whether or not you are going to accept this view of language education. However, we can probably all agree that there is at least some truth in the descriptions given. To illustrate some of the things that might be called inadequate language education, I briefly sketch a few situations that I have observed.

ACTIVITY

In each situation below, decide on the pros and cons of the action or activity, and suggest alternatives or improvements if appropriate.

6d

1. *To aid in the development of the students' vocabulary, a high school institutes a 'word of the day' activity. Every day a word is chosen more or less at random from Webster's dictionary, and this is printed in the daily bulletin, and/or announced on the intercom. 'Today's word is: <u>judgement</u>'. In every class this word is supposed to be defined, exemplified, and discussed.*

2. *You walk past the window of an ESL class in an adult school which has a reputation of being the best and most innovative school in the area. You see a teacher writing down on the blackboard a number of words that all have the letter combination ai in them: straight, braid, paid, wait, etc. All students, many of them apparently recent immigrants and working people, sit at individual desks writing down the words in their notebook. You don't have time to investigate further, you can't hear what the teacher says, if anything, and in any case, you don't want to seem too nosy.*

3. *Every week Brian comes home from fifth grade with a list of 20 vocabulary words which he has to write out three times each; then, for each word, he has to write a sentence in which that word is used. Every Friday there is a spelling test on these 20 words.*

4. *In a conversation lesson in Spanish (translated here into English, for the sake of convenience), classroom interaction is along the lines suggested by the following extract:*
    Teacher: Did you go anywhere during the long weekend, Sam?
    Sam: I wen – eh to eh I wento Puebla with my uncle.
    Teacher: Oh, great! To Puebla! And you, Joyce, did you go anywhere?
    Joyce: No, I stay home.
    Teacher: Ah, you stayed at home. Very good.
This continues until all students have had at least one turn to say what they did or where they went.

(Author's data)

In these examples, all based on actual experiences, the focus is on language in one way or another. The question is if, in the spirit of language awareness, we can come up with more exciting and meaningful language work that is integrative, creative, stimulates thinking and assists in learning in a multifaceted way. Would formal linguistic training, as appears to be suggested by Baron, be the appropriate teacher preparation for this? Or would this merely turn the teacher into one of the 'codifying and legitimizing' grammarians that Bourdieu talks about, in which case we have leapt from the frying pan into the fire?

Halliday has the following to say about linguistic courses for teachers:

I would like to reject categorically the assertion that a course of general linguistics is of no particular use to teachers. I think it's fundamental. But I don't think it should be a sort of watered down academic linguistic course. It should be something new, designed and worked out by linguists and teachers together (Halliday, 1982 page 13).

This quote embodies two underlying assumptions: first, the idea that (at least) some people view linguistics training as useless for teachers, and second, that linguistics training is essential, but will only work if done in a special way.

In a research project conducted in Hampshire schools (in Great Britain), Mitchell and Hooper found similar tendencies. They interviewed teachers of English and modern languages, finding that many had little or no formal linguistic training (thus confirming Baron's statement above), and those that had had such training found it virtually useless, if they remembered anything from it at all. However, there were also some indications of a felt need for knowledge, or some dissatisfaction with the depth of language education they were able to engage in, and perhaps some defensiveness about the teacher's own lack of language knowledge.

On the other side of the coin, the British National Curriculum has spurred in-service training for teachers as part of the LINC Project (Language in the National Curriculum, see Carter 1990), and a number of innovative language-awareness projects in elementary schools are reported, by the teachers themselves, in a fascinating collection of classroom case studies (Bain, Fitzgerald and Taylor, 1992). These projects go across the curriculum, address both spoken and written language, and study language diversity.

6.3   Classroom interaction

At the beginning of the chapter I emphasized that language is central in education at many different levels. Nowhere is this centrality more evident, however, than in the classroom where learning is carried out in interactions between teacher and students. To analyse how this interaction takes place, let's have a closer look at another ESL transcript. As before, we note certain differences between the classroom interaction and the conversation, relating to such things as who decides who speaks to whom about what, the predictability of what may happen next, and in general the issue of control, which appears to reside unilaterally in the teacher.

6e
1 *A: How many people are talking. Elly? . . . How many people?*
2 *B: Two people.*
3 *A: Yes, that's right, two people. And what are these two people talking about. Marcia.*
4 *C: (unintelligible) people ask the way.*
5 *A: Uhuh.*
(Author's data)

   How is this control manifested, and how does it promote (or inhibit!) learning? To obtain an answer, we need to do a little bit of **discourse analysis**.

ACTIVITY

6f
1. *First of all, divide extract **6e** into two equal (symmetrical) parts, by drawing a vertical line between two words.*
Where did you draw the line?

Between _____ *and* _____ .

2. *You now have two exchanges of three units (let's call them moves) each. Try to give names to each of these moves (in terms of what they do, or their function):*

1. _____
2. _____
3. _____

If I have succeeded in guiding you to the correct analysis, you drew a line between people and And in turn 3, and you called the three moves in each exchange something like (1) question, elicitation, or initiation (2) answer or response, and (3) evaluation or feedback. Each set of three turns can be called an exchange, and the whole extract thus consists of two full exchanges of question–answer–evaluation (in the literature this is often referred to as the IRF exchange, for Initiation–Response–Follow-up). The switch-over from exchange 1 to exchange 2 occurs right in the middle of the teacher's turn, without a pause. Now answer one more question.

3. *Whenever a student speaks, what is the reason why that student speaks? And, related to that, is there a place anywhere in this extract for students to produce some talk spontaneously, on their own initiative?*

(Author's data)

I fully expect question 3 to come across as a rhetorical one. Students only speak when nominated by, or given a turn by, the teacher. And then every turn by a student is vetted by the teacher, so that the student turn is sandwiched between two teacher turns. Finally, the switch-over from addressing one student to addressing the next student occurs seamlessly in the middle of a teacher turn, so that the student has, to quote Dudley Moore, no chance to get a word in edgeways. The exchange system illustrated here is thus virtually interruption-proof. This design no doubt works wonders for orderly classroom behaviour, for discipline and for observance of the rule: 'Only one person speaks at a time.' However, the unfortunate side-effect is that spontaneous talk, initiative, volunteering ideas, true conversation, becomes impossible in this system.

How much of classroom talk is of this nature? What other kinds of interaction are possible, and how are they practised? These are important questions for language awareness, but there are many others which we do not have the time to discuss in detail. Let me just list some, to simulate discussion and further research:

— In a foreign language lesson, teachers often use the native language some of the time, and the target language some of the time. Are some general guidelines possible for the use of the target/native language, and what kinds of rationale can be found in the classroom for the switching that occurs?

— In foreign-language group work, students often use the native language to facilitate the logistics of a task and to give quick checks and feedback on what is to be done. Should such native language use be tolerated or banned?

— In group work in general, students often come to a quick consensus and go along with whatever seems most likely to produce the results the teacher wants, in order to achieve early closure and get the task over with, rather than to solve the problem in the best way possible. Can anything be done about that?

— Both teacher and students are concerned that the students speak correctly. How can teachers correct, or students be corrected, without turning the talk into artificial talk, or discouraging the students from continuing to speak voluntarily? Or should teachers perhaps not correct any formal errors at all, since parents do not usually correct their small children?

6.4   Textbooks

N. S. Prabhu, who pioneered task-based language teaching in Bangalore, India, said that a syllabus, the actual content and procedures of lessons (including the materials), should be simple, because a complex or complete syllabus, containing everything one might want or need, actually 'reduces the range of language that can be used in teaching materials or the classroom' (*Second Language Pedagogy* (1987), page 92). It often happens that interesting issues come up in the classroom, or students find news items or clippings of topical interest, and after some brief discussion the teacher, reluctantly perhaps, says: 'Anyway, let's get back to the lesson; we haven't finished page forty-three yet.' At such moments the syllabus feels like a straitjacket which constrains movement and freedom, and which forces attention away from relevant and motivating material back to the known and predictable tedium of 'the book'.

No doubt teachers often have little choice but to 'stick to the syllabus': it may be narrowly prescribed what has to be 'covered', and perhaps there will be a mandatory test to check that everything that has been covered was in fact retained in a regurgitable way. But we have to ask ourselves if, in our zeal to 'cover' everything, we perhaps fail to 'uncover' many more things, and if instead of stimulating learning we induce periodic regurgitation.

In many school systems, subject-matter teaching operates on the basis of oversized, overweight textbooks, which cover everything from cover to cover. In the US, these books are so heavy that three of them would not fit in an average backpack, and even if they did, they might cause the hapless student serious back injury. As a result, many schools are forced to acquire two sets, one to keep at school, another to keep at home. This expenditure, excessive in my view (though publishers no doubt like to claim otherwise, and parents may sense some security in the sheer bulk and reassuring banality of the text), prevents schools from investing in efficient, flexible and motivating materials that allow students to engage with relevant materials in meaningful ways. At their worst such textbooks turn into turgid tomes that leave nothing to the imagination. Given that they must be acceptable to everyone, they tend to be so bland and uncritically conformist, that any thinking person is immediately turned off by them. Let me just quote one sentence from one such textbook to show how meaningless and unreal they tend to be:

The economic gap between workers and owners has narrowed almost to the point of extinction, especially in the United States.

This extraordinary piece of information can be found in Magruder's *American Government*, Revised by W. A. McClenaghan (1987), Allyn and Bacon. On page 22.

There is no need just to single out the venerable Magruder, either. The point is a quite general one, and it is that any textbook, to be acceptable to a wide market, and to cover a full curriculum, has made so many compromises between inception and publication that it can hardly be fit for use in a democratic, enlightened educational setting. It is almost of necessity insulting to any clear-thinking person, whether child or adult. Perhaps the most extraordinary – and frightening – thought is that there may actually be teachers and students who have become so numbed by years of uncritical consumption of such materials, that they don't even notice anything wrong with the quoted statement or others like it.

Textbooks for language teaching are slightly less constrained in terms of subject matter, since they are all in a foreign language, and anything that doesn't look quite 'normal' can be excused since it relates to a foreign culture. Even so, many foreign language textbooks go out of their way to be nondescript, perhaps to make sure the focus stays squarely on the grammar, rather than straying to content. So, here another aspect of the 'covering' urge manifests itself: such textbooks look at the target language as a product, itemized and inventoried, and proceed to 'cover' as much as possible in successive lessons. Language exploration, using the real world as a textbook, is thus made impossible.

Perhaps now, with the availability of multi-media packages, CD-ROM and other computer and video software, the era of the generic textbook will come to an end. Certainly, already there are signs that innovative publishers are combining textbooks with a greater variety of more flexible, mixed-media materials of a thematic and task-based nature.

When language awareness guides our teaching and learning, we will in most cases still need textbooks, though perhaps much thinner and more flexible ones. However, our real, main textbook will be the world of language use all around us in the street, the electronic media, newspapers, novels, and so on. Becoming aware, the student and the teacher find instances of language use to discuss and analyse, to learn from and to enrich their critical understanding of the world and to become better language users themselves, more in control of the medium, and therefore the message.

In this chapter I have focused on language awareness in education. I have argued that language permeates education to such a degree that, to understand educational processes and to make meaningful changes, a deep understanding of the various roles of language is essential. We do not get such understanding from the study of grammar books, theoretical linguistics, or textbooks of various kinds. Rather, we need to become aware of the way we use language, and the way it is used around us, in schools and classrooms, in textbooks and staff development meetings. When we become aware, we can stop taking whatever happens for granted, and we can begin thinking about meaningful changes.

Seeing clearly, thinking clearly and speaking clearly are related. And these are related to good pedagogy, and good pedagogy promotes critical, autonomous and responsible thinking and working. Empowerment is not possible otherwise, and in this spirit I argue that language awareness can actually be the key to true educational reform.

PROJECT

The best place to start investigating language awareness in education is by examining classroom talk. To do this, it is worth first consulting books such as Dick Allwright's and Kathi Bailey's *Focus on the Language Classroom* (1991), or Ruth Wajnrayb's *Classroom Observation Tasks* (1993), both of which contain a variety of suggestions for projects on classroom talk. For detailed and meticulous work it will be necessary to record a lesson and transcribe it, although there are also a large number of different coding systems especially developed to look at a particular features of classroom interaction. Another option, if you are a practising teacher, is to do a peer coaching project, in which you team up with a partner to observe each other's classes in accordance with a 'contract' stating what features of your lesson you wish your partner to observe (and vice versa), and conversations about the lessons afterwards.

SUMMARY

- Language fulfils a variety of roles in education across the entire curriculum. It is central to the functioning of education, not only in the classroom, but in all other school-related contexts as well.
- Classroom language use is quite different to language use in other settings, such as general conversation. Teacher talk, if it is limited to traditional formats such as the IRF exchange, may control and limit the options for speaking and creativity of students, and it is useful for teachers to examine a variety of ways of interacting with students.

- There is a perennial struggle in education between a focus on language in terms of 'correct' form (pronunciation, grammar, punctuation etc) and a focus on meaningful communication and personal enrichment.
- Textbooks tend to limit the range of language and topics that can be discussed in the classroom, and often put a damper on the students' intrinsic motivation. They 'cover' rather than 'uncover'.

7 Critical language issues

Critical theory is a term that is used quite frequently these days. One sees it in sociology, pedagogy, even science in general. It is the third phase in Jerome Ravetz's historical overview, *Scientific Knowledge and Its Social Problems* (1971), which sees science moving from <u>academic</u> (science for the sake of science) to <u>industrial</u> (science for profit, research and development, technology), to <u>critical</u> (science to assist in the solution of perennial human problems). Critical language awareness (also critical discourse analysis) should thus be seen as part of that general movement towards a more critical science. As far as language and pedagogy are concerned, the critical movement is influenced, among others, by the work of Brazilian educator Paulo Freire *Pedagogy of the Oppressed* (1972), German social philosopher Jürgen Habermas *The Theory of Communicative Action* (1984), and French sociologist Pierre Bourdieu *Language and Symbolic Power* (1991). Current researchers and writers in this area include Norman Fairclough, David Corson, Michael Apple and Ira Shor.

In education, critical theory has espoused such concepts as empowerment, equity, multiculturalism and critical thinking, and is centrally concerned with the issue of power and control. The relationship between language and power has been discussed in such books as Dwight Bolinger's *Language, the Loaded Weapon*, and, more recently, Norman Fairclough's *Language and Power*, (1989) and Pierre Bourdieu's *Language and Symbolic Power*. How classroom language can be controlling I illustrated in the last chapter, when we looked at an extract of teacher–student interaction.

In general it is probably fair to say that in schools there is a tendency towards making students conform to a perceived status quo, and towards the enforcement of codes of behaviour and discipline. In the words of Michael Foucault, the aim of the school as an institution embodying a 'disciplinary technology' is to forge a 'docile body that may be subjected, used, transformed and improved' (Rabinow *A Foucault Reader*, page 17). In a school, students learn to behave in a way that is appropriate in schools, and this is different from the way it is proper to behave in other places, like fast-food restaurants, churches, or casinos. Every place has its own 'decorum' which a competent and decent visitor observes. To illustrate this, here is a little quiz based on a sentence from a book by Ellen Langer (*Mindfulness* (1989), page 35). Try to match the words on the left with those on the right, and then read the sentence in the appendix.

ACTIVITY

7a

whisper	*police stations*
be anxious	*schools*
be sad	*parties*
be docile	*hospitals*
be jovial	*cemeteries*

(adapted from Langer 1989)

In schools, then, we are supposed to be docile. What does this mean for our progressive and innovative attempts to promote creativity, initiative, autonomy, critical thinking and all the rest? The question is not easily answered and before even trying to answer it, we need to investigate the reality of the school and, indeed, the workplace and any other place which is important to us. This investigation, of course, must include centrally the investigation of patterns of language use in the chosen settings, so that we become aware of what is going on, begin to understand the processes at work, and then start working on innovations.

In the past chapters I have several times touched upon critical issues such as correctness, classroom talk and routine. However, so far I have treated these mainly as sharp edges to an otherwise straightforward (non-critical) discussion. We will now look at some critical issues in more detail. We will again move into the classroom, but we will also examine other discourse worlds to see how language is involved in shaping them. In order to get familiar with some of the basic terminology relating to critical language study, you may like to try the fill-in-the-blank exercise below.

ACTIVITY

7b

Culture words

1. *A profession, a trade, an interest group etc, often creates its own special language, or _____ .*

2. *People that are _____ think that their own culture, language, or way of life is better than any other.*

3. *'An unreasonable fear and dislike of foreigners or strangers' is called _____ .*

4. *Meaningless but important-sounding official language is often called _____ .*

5. *Language that is not usually acceptable in formal settings, but that may be used among close friends or in peer groups, is called _____ .*

6. *Some words, especially those denoting bodily functions, sexual activities or organs, religious topics and diseases or death, are _____ . They are often replaced by _____ .*

7. *The distinction between a _____ and a language is often based on political and social criteria rather than linguistic ones.*

8. *The term _____ refers to a lack of cultural identity which may be characterized by disorientation, anxiety and isolation, and an absence of normative standards of conduct and belief.*

Use these words: *gobbledygook – dialect – jargon – euphemism – anomie – ethnocentric – taboo – xenophobia – slang*

(Author's data)

7.1 The weird, the warped and the normal

Language has the power to make strange things normal and, much more rarely, normal things strange. Conversation in particular, through the comfortable familiarity of its format, can have a powerful normalizing effect on the things being discussed. But the same can be done through advertising, especially when it is repeated with some frequency. 'What I tell you three times is true,' said the Bellman in Lewis Carroll's poem *The Hunting of the Snark*. Analogously, we might say that 'what we talk about for a while becomes normal.'

As an example, one of the things foreigners find hard to understand about the US is the obsession with guns, their easy availability, and the amount of murder and accidental death that occurs through the use of guns. These foreigners may be amazed to hear an announcement on the radio like the following, though Americans, whether they are for or against open sales of guns, may hardly notice it. The voice announces a weekend gun show in a nearby fairground, saying that all kinds of guns, knives and other weapons, including collectors' items, will be on display and for sale. The ad concludes:

'It's a great family event – you'll find something for everyone!'

By treating the gun show in the same way as any other family outing, a fair, a concert, a picnic, or whatever, it attains a normality that makes listeners accept it as a quite ordinary affair, one which you do not think twice about.

A similar effect is obtained at gambling casinos when harmless names are given to chips of values like a hundred, five hundred, or a thousand dollars each. A mere $25 chip, for example, is called 'a quarter', and who would worry about spending a few quarters?

Talking about things as if they were normal actually has the effect of normalizing the things in question. This may well be one of the most powerful functions of language, functioning to create cultures, tie groups together, make the unknown familiar and the frightening bearable, and justify some of the strangest and most unjustifiable activities.

7.2 Prejudice

—In his book on language awareness, Eric Hawkins reports a white Leicestershire schoolgirl as saying 'You can't even go to the bathroom without hearing those Indian girls jabbering away in their stupid Punjabi language.'

—In a recent court case, a judge awarded a California company the right to order Hispanic workers who had been speaking Spanish on the job to speak English. Anglo workers had complained that these Hispanic workers were making fun of them in Spanish.

—On a radio commercial mention was made of the '400 dialects of India'. (One does not hear English, French, or Dutch being referred to as 'dialects of Europe' – those are languages).

What do these examples have in common? They all refer to some languages as being legitimate, others not (or less so). What determines the legitimacy of a particular language? The answer to this question is extremely complex, since legitimacy depends on a wide range of variable factors, largely determined by context. The main parameters determining legitimacy involve geographical, social, historical, racial, economic and political factors. In the case of the Leicestershire schoolgirl, her own language, if it is a regional English dialect, might well be called a 'stupid Leicestershire accent' if it were heard in a school in Surrey. The Hispanic workers' Spanish, outlawed in a California factory, is enforced in countless schools in Latin America for children whose native language is Aymara, Quechua, Aguaruna, Guarani, Nahuatl and so on. These latter languages are routinely called dialects by speakers of major European languages. Yet, Aymara is no more a dialect than French is.

We all have specific ideas about or attitudes towards different groups (nationalities, races) and the languages they speak. This is inevitable, though it is often denied or ignored, and the very idea that prejudice is something we all may succumb to may be violently rejected. Thus, a few years ago a debate raged in educational circles in the US about whether children of different ethnicities should be disciplined in different ways in early schooling, because they are used to different patterns in their cultures and at home: some children are gently reasoned with when they do something wrong, other are yelled at, yet others spanked with or without the aid of belts or broomsticks. The reader may imagine what the class list of a multicultural classroom might look like if some advocates of differential discipline had their way:

Joshua: yell at loudly
Maria: spank bottom three times
Willie: talk to softly
Zachary: lock in dark closet . . . and so on.

At some point in this debate (reported in detail in various newspapers), one State educational official, an African-American, remarked that everyone, himself included, had inherent racist tendencies which they had to be aware of and consciously fight against. Upon which another prominent official, an Anglo-American, retorted that the earlier speaker, since he admitted to being a racist, should resign immediately. It would be difficult to find children in a racially mixed kindergarten carrying on in such ridiculous ways.

We all have our prejudices, even though at times we may pretend that we don't. Prejudice (and the closely related activity of stereotyping) is, in general, related to ignorance, so that creating an awareness of those prejudices that we do have, and then increasing our knowledge and understanding of the objects of our prejudices, can be an effective method to promote cross-cultural understanding. The exercise below is designed to be one step in such a general process of promoting understanding. I have done this exercise, or variants of it, with several classes, and perhaps should sound a warning. Like the magician on TV who saws a woman in half and warns the audience 'Do not try this trick at home', just taking such an exercise into any classroom without careful preparation and a solid understanding of the students and what they can handle, can be disastrous (for an example, see 'backfiring' below).

ACTIVITY

7c

Who has stereotypes?

In the spaces below, write any nationality or ethnic group that people think of in your environment for each descriptor. If no appropriate group comes to mind, leave the space blank. When you have finished, circle the adjectives that were easiest to complete. This exercise is <u>anonymous</u> – do not put your name on the paper.

Examples:

43. *taciturn   Estonians*
56. (*rich*)   *Liechtensteiners*

---

1. *serious* _____	11. *romantic* _____
2. *lazy* _____	12. *shrewd* _____
3. *fun-loving* _____	13. *intelligent* _____
4. *hard-working* _____	14. *stingy* _____
5. *aggressive* _____	15. *untrustworthy* _____
6. *humourless* _____	16. *loud* _____
7. *honest* _____	17. *artistic* _____
8. *emotional* _____	18. *narrow-minded* _____
9. *boastful* _____	19. *smelly* _____
10. *drunk* _____	20. *stupid* _____

(Author's data)

On occasion, I have asked large groups of students to do this exercise, and have tabulated the results to show and discuss the general patterns that emerge. It turns out that, with US students, the French and Italians are clear winners in the 'romantic' category, and in a class some years ago, Russians were the unfortunate leaders in the 'humourless' category (this may have changed in the last few years). When I asked that particular class, however, how many students knew or had ever talked to a Russian, the answer was no one. Such a finding naturally allows us to investigate where a prejudice may come from, and how it is related to ignorance. In this particular case, the stereotype reflects the way Russians have traditionally been portrayed in the media and in Hollywood movies.

7.2.1   When things backfire

I suggested in the above 'prejudice' task that it is necessary to know the students quite well, and to prepare the ground carefully, before implementing tasks that delve into people's tacitly held attitudes. Things might otherwise get out of hand, and the class might come to be controlled by prejudicial sentiments (rather than being in control of them), every utterance taking one step further away from common sense and decency, until the purpose of the activity is lost from sight. This appears to have happened in the classroom episode described in the extract from Larry Meeks's column below. You may reflect on what might be the most appropriate response of the various parties involved, including the teacher, the principal and the 'appalled Mom'. Do you agree with Larry Meeks's advice?

Teacher should reassess project that backfired

LARRY MEEKS

Dear Larry: I am a white mother with a daughter in the eighth-grade. My daughter's teacher assigned a creative activity that was to be performed orally in class.

Each student was given a sheet of paper with outlines of four human heads. In each head was a detailed picture of the brain. The first picture showed a head full of brains. The second had a lesser amount, the third less still, and the fourth had the smallest amount of brains. All the students were required to give a name to each picture.

When my daughter was called for her answer, she said out loud, "genius, smart, ignorant and dumb." Another student said, "Hillary Clinton, the Clinton daughter, the Clinton cat and President Clinton." Another said, "father, brother, sister and mother." Everyone was laughing and having a good time being creative. Each student tried to be funnier and more creative than his classmates. Finally one student named the figures, "Asian, white, black and Hispanic." The children laughed louder. Even the teacher laughed.

My daughter told me the above story, with the comment that it is not nice to laugh at racist remarks. I totally concur with my daughter and told her so. However, I do not know what to say or do about the situation at school.

Please answer soon. I do not want the situation to pass, but want to act in a responsible manner. — Appalled Mom

Dear Appalled Mom: I am assuming the teacher had good intentions but allowed the situation to get out of control. It is all right to be creative but not disrespectful, obnoxious, sexist or racist. The situation could have been avoided if the teacher had set parameters on the assignment at the beginning disallowing such comments.

Contact the principal and report the incident. The teacher should be required to reteach the assignment with the proper restrictions and admonitions for proper behavior. If you are afraid to comment, send the principal a copy of this column, with the name of the teacher. Let me know the re-sults.

(*Californian Extra*, 5 October 1993)

7.3 Bilingualism

The most commonly asked question about **bilingualism** is whether
it is a good idea to raise children bilingually, for example in
families where both parents speak a different native language.
Once the parents are convinced that it would indeed be beneficial
for the child in the long run, the next question is what the best
method would be to go about this. Many experts advocate the so-
called one parent, one language method, in which each parent
speaks to the child only in his or her native language so that for
example, the child only hears Spanish from the mother, and English
from the father. The strictness with which this rule is maintained
varies, and the views about whether or not this matters also vary.
Sometimes children in such a situation begin to speak later than
others, but they appear to catch up pretty quickly. Generally it is
believed that bilingual children acquire a greater degree of cognitive
flexibility, and they may also develop more and earlier **meta**linguistic awareness (awareness about language). Earlier views that bilingualism leads to retardation and various kinds of mental deficiency
are thus entirely unfounded, even though one still hears comments
to this effect from time to time. At a conservative estimate, bilingual
children are at least equal to monolingual children in all academic
and emotional respects, but we must not forget, of course, that
they have made one enormous gain: they know two languages
instead of one!

In arguments for or against bilingual education the onus is often
put on the advocates of bilingualism to prove that these children
do the same or better than monolingual children in the second
language. It is conveniently forgotten that an equally important
measure ought to be how well they are doing in their native
language. After all, the possession of an additional language is an
important good.

More importantly, however, I would argue very strongly that

every child has the right to speak, maintain and develop his or her mother tongue, regardless of all other educational concerns, and that an equitable educational system has the duty to support this right actively. This is extremely important for the child's emotional and cognitive development, as well as for the health of the family. Very often in many countries minority-language children are taught in the dominant language only, and this puts before them a choice between two worlds: the world of the home, or the world of the school. If they choose the former, they drop out of school, and if they choose the latter they drop out of the family (many may drop out of both, and fall into gangs). These children are forced to make a choice long before they are ready to do so, before either the first or the second language has been fully developed. They therefore gain one language and lose the other. There is not room for both in such a scenario. This is known as subtractive bilingualism.

There is a related issue to this which concerns the different cultural, social and economic perspectives of the home and the school, and which often creates a double bind, that is, conflicting messages between which it is impossible to choose. I can best illustrate this with an example from my fieldwork in the Peruvian Andes.

In the Altiplano, five-year-old children fulfil a variety of essential tasks in the family: look after siblings, cook, fetch water, help in the market, watch the animals. When they go to the Spanish-speaking, Spanish-culture school, they get the implicit message that those activities don't count, since they interfere with the school work. Worse, they are detrimental to academic progress. Thus, school socialization clashes head-on with home socialization, and there is not really a happy way out. The child receives multiple messages, as follows:

(Mother):   Do your best in school!
(Father):   Help your mother!
(Teacher): Don't be lazy!
                  and so on.

The child might try to reason as follows:

We are poor, so I must help my family.
We are poor, so I must study to make a better future for myself
  and my family.
If I study, I cannot help my family now.
We will become poorer.
If I help my family now, I cannot study.
We will always be poor.
Whatever I do, we will be poor.

In the political arguments over bilingual education it is the child whose experiences and interests come last. Hypothetical or statistically manufactured outcomes and financial balance sheets are the chips in the game, but the quality of the educational experience, the long-term emotional well-being, the memories of the school, the richness of interactions with others and the significance of friendships, all these intangibles, invisible to committee reports, but crucial when the real human balance is drawn up over the long run, vanish completely from the conference table and the auditorium lectern.

A critical language perspective on bilingualism and bilingual education might work to refocus the debate radically. Rather than looking at test scores, experimental groups and control groups, interaction indices and average daily attendance, it might look at the school and the classroom in terms of the opportunities for learning it presents, the memorable occasions that are created, and how happy the child feels in it. The fact that we do not have convenient research methods to quantify and measure vague notions such as 'memorable' and 'happy', does not diminish their importance. As a prominent financial commentator said on the radio about consumer confidence, 'The fact that you cannot count it does not mean that it doesn't count'.

7.4 Language policy

Since language is such an important part of social life and institutions, governments often consciously try to influence linguistic issues, such as which language will be used for official government business, which language will be used in schools, whether there will be just one or more officially recognized languages in the country, what the 'standard' version will be in terms of grammar, vocabulary and pronunciation and many other similar questions. In addition, watchdog institutions may be set up to prevent the deterioration of the language, for example by means of discouraging or banning the use of borrowed words from other languages. The French Académie Française, and the Spanish Academia Real, are two venerable institutions of this type, but whether they succeed in stemming the tide of lexical invasion, particularly from English, is very much in doubt.

Another way in which authorities may try to induce linguistic changes (or prevent them) is by language planning. A newly-independent country, for instance, may want to establish its own official language, either resuscitated from an ancient tongue (as happened in Israel with Hebrew), chosen from among a range of local languages to replace a no longer wanted colonial language (Bahasa Indonesia, Bahasa Malaysia), or choose a national language from among local dialects (Norway). Sometimes such efforts are relatively successful, as in the examples mentioned, other times they may fail. Many languages have disappeared in the past, and continue to do so, whether by 'murder' or 'suicide' (Hoffman, *Bilingualism* (1991)) is often hard to tell. It is clear that linguistic oppression has occurred and continues to occur in many places, and in many shapes or forms.

In chapter 1, I mentioned the role of language in the British National Curriculum, which began to be implemented in 1989. As a national policy, the British government explicitly promoted knowledge about language as an educational objective across the curriculum. However, advocates of language awareness may have different views on the methods and purposes of courses for knowledge about language. For example, the LINC (Language In the National Curriculum) materials developed by Ron Carter and associates take a creative and critical view of language but, although they were commissioned by the government, they were summarily rejected since they failed to fulfil the view of language education held by the people in power: instruction in formal grammar and correct speaking and writing, as the following quote illustrates:

... we've allowed so many standards to slip ... teachers weren't bothering to teach kids to spell and to punctuate properly ... if you allow standards to slip to the stage where good English is no better than bad English, where people turn up filthy ... at school ... all those things cause people to have no standards at all, and once you lose standards then there's no imperative to stay out of crime. (Norman Tebbit, Radio 4, 1985. Quoted in Carter, 1992).

It is interesting to trace the causal chain imputed here by Mr Tebbit:

teach spelling and punctuation $\longrightarrow$ good English $\longrightarrow$ standards $\longrightarrow$ stay out of crime

Language policy, then, may enforce or promote certain ways of teaching language in the schools, in order to produce citizens that conform to a certain model. This applies also to bilingual education, where the goal is to produce citizens who speak the dominant language. In the views of many people, for example, those who belong to the 'US English' movement in the US, this can only be achieved if the child's native language is kept out of the school system as much as possible, even if this means that this child will lose the native language (subtractive bilingualism, or replacing one language with another – see also the preceding section). At the same time, the learning of foreign languages is regarded as a useful academic goal. If such views were to prevail, we might see a school system which promotes <u>unlearning</u> native languages, while at the same time promoting <u>learning</u> foreign languages.

In contradiction to US English and similar views, most (in fact the vast majority) of specialists in bilingualism and bilingual education agree that a solid grounding in the native language is the best springboard for second language acquisition. Moreover, the argument that the more exposure a child has to target language, the faster the acquisition will be, is simplistic: if the exposure is of low quality (uninteresting, alienating, incomprehensible etc), simply increasing it will do more harm than good. If the exposure is of high quality and is perceived in an emotionally positive way, small quantities will suffice for language acquisition to occur in an optimal way. However, as the literature clearly shows, the debate about bilingual education is often informed by political expediency, xenophobia and self-interest, rather than by solid educational arguments.

Language policy and language planning are, in practice, determined by a very wide range of social, economic and political factors, and success or failure are therefore only partly under the control of the professionals who draw up the plans and implement the policies.

7.5 Voice

Traditional psycholinguistic views of language use depict it as originating in a thought or idea which is encoded in language, transmitted over the airwaves, received by the listener, decoded and interpreted, and mentally processed into thoughts or ideas similar to (if transmission was successful) those the originator started out with. In a very simple sense this is of course correct, in the same way that it is correct to describe a game of chess as people pushing small pieces of wood across a board.

However, just as a chess game involves much more than the

movement of small pieces of wood, speaking is much more than the transmission of information over the air. Every act of speaking carries various <u>points of view</u>, or 'voices' as the Russian linguist Bakhtin put it. In a conversation, as we have seen in earlier chapters, an utterance is contingent on previous and following utterances, and can therefore not be understood or explained without reference to the entire speech context or discourse. An individual speaker speaks through a social language (Wertsch *Voices of the Mind* (1991), page 58) which he or she has appropriated. As Bakhtin says, 'The word in language is half someone else's. It becomes 'one's own' only when the speaker populates it with his own intention, his own accent, when he appropriates the word, adapting it to his own semantic and expressive intention' (Bakhtin *The Dialogic Imagination* (1981), page 293). Critical language study differs from traditional linguistics in that it examines language in this light, as a multiplicity of voices wrapped up in acts of saying.

When the radio commercial (see above) announced that the gun show was a 'family event', and that one could 'find something for everyone', one could identify multiple voices at work, as well as multiple originators ('speakers') and audiences.

speakers:
— organizers of gun show
— writers of advertising copy
— speaker on the radio

audience:
— people interested in guns
— general public

points of view:
— information: date, place
— gun shows are for the whole family (not just gun nuts)
— gun shows are 'normal' and 'friendly'
— gun shows are co-classified with antique shows, county fairs, etc

Similarly, in a classroom the dialogue between teacher and student carries more than one voice, which becomes particularly noticeable when 'conversation' occurs. The teacher has to be simultaneously participant and expert, equal partner and authority, language user and language evaluator. The student has to be participant and displayer of competence. This can lead to conflicts in the language use, so that the voices enacted in the dialogue become conflicting instead of harmonious. We can see this in various ways in the classroom extracts used in this last chapter. It is also striking in oral proficiency interviews, when the interviewer wants to elicit conversational language use. As I found in a series of experiments (van Lier *Oral Proficiency Interviews as Conversation* (1989)), it is very hard to reconcile interviewing with conversing. For example, when the interviewer asked me, as part of the warm-up, such questions as 'Where do you live,' and 'How do you like it,' I would, for experimental reasons, answer back like this: 'In Salinas, and where do you live?', 'It's quite nice, and how about you? Do you have any kids?' When I asked counter-questions like this, something that is expected, indeed required in polite conversation, the interviewer was visibly taken aback and the interview process unravelled. It seems that, in the very display of my conversational competence, I wrested away the control and the power from the interviewer, I wreaked havoc with the planned progression of the interview along its well-oiled grooves of level checks, probes and so on. The voices of conversation and the voices of interviewing (as a form of testing) appeared to be incompatible with one another.

These are not unimportant, idiosyncratic frills and bumps on the surface of a rule-governed linguistic system, that can therefore be ignored in the theoretical study of grammar. In the view of critical linguistics, issues of voice and the contingency of linguistic utterances go to the very heart of grammar. Without them, language study turns into trivial pursuit, and language itself can never be understood.

*

In this final chapter we have looked at language awareness from a critical perspective. In this perspective, it is not sufficient to understand language in a formal sense in terms of grammatical rules, definitions of words, spelling and pronunciation, in short, in terms of 'correct' language; rather we must understand language in terms of its place in social life. Multiculturalism, prejudice and stereotyping, bilingualism, the normalizing function of language, language policy and voicing, these are all issues which theoretical linguistics is practically silent about, but which critical language awareness aims to illuminate.

If we want to use language awareness to assist in the solution of social problems, for educational innovation and to become more in control of our own place in the world, formal knowledge, such as that illustrated in chapters 2 and 3 of this book, and such as is contained in grammar books, linguistics texts and dictionaries, is essential, but unless we are able to transcend that formal knowledge itself, it will be of little use.

PROJECT

Investigate an area in which the power of language is relevant. Collect relevant data and write an essay. Some suitable topics:
— the phenomenon of 'political correctness'.
— the relationship between schooling and democracy.
— the media (for example, how anchor and co-anchor (usually male and female) use social chat as part of the news broadcast).
— areas of traditional inequality, such as gender, race, class.
— language in advertising.

SUMMARY

- Critical language awareness is part of a general trend in the social sciences called critical theory, which stresses the social responsibility of scientists to assist in the solution of pressing problems.

- Critical theory deals with issues of power and control, and the role that language plays in these issues.
- Language is part of what defines a particular context or institution, such as education, and often serves to make strange things familiar.
- Prejudice and stereotypes tend to be based on ignorance, and awareness raising is therefore one step towards promoting cross-cultural understanding.
- Bilingualism and bilingual education are controversial issues in many countries, through critical theorists would argue that every child has the right to develop and maintain its mother tongue, and that educational institutions have the duty to assist the child in this respect.
- Language policy and language planning often include specific measures to adopt one official language among several spoken in a country, to revive languages that are in decline, to safeguard a standard language among various dialects, or to set standards of correctness and 'proper' usage in the schools.
- When we speak, our language may reflect a range of voices, our own as well as others', whether it be roles such as 'concerned father' or 'friendly neighbour' or 'tough teacher', or a sensitivity towards those we are addressing. Language thus has multiple meanings, often with a wide range of potential interpretations which go well beyond the literal meanings of the words spoken.

Key to activities

This key contains suggestions for answers to those activities which are not explained in the text itself and which are marked with an asterisk. These are often not the only possible answers, but may be used as guidance.

CHAPTER 1

Page 7

1: F Chapter 5 will show that things are not as clear-cut as that.
2: F Many dialects do have a written form, and there are also many languages without a written form.
3: F Exposure is useless if you don't pay attention to it, or if for some reason you cannot relate to it.
4: T Languages, as long as they have living speakers, will keep changing.
5: F The notion 'substandard' is not accepted in linguistics. The only thing that is 'superior' about a standard dialect/language is that it has been promoted to 'official' status.
6: F All languages borrow, and this makes the language richer.
7: F/T A language may sound more or less beautiful to you, but you will find that many people will disagree with you. Beauty is entirely in the ear and mouth of the user, it is not a linguistic quality.
8: F In themselves words are neither clean nor dirty, they are just words. Speakers give the words connotations.
9: F Most dictionaries and grammars will (eventually!) include a form if enough speakers use it consistently.
10: F There is nothing logical about the fact that *I asked him a question* is considered correct and *I explained him the answer* is considered incorrect, and numerous other rules like that.

CHAPTER 2

Page 20
1. A is further to the front and B is further to the back of the palate.
2. A is aspirated and B is not.
3. the n in B turns into [ŋ].
4. depending on your dialect, the tt in B may sound like [d].
5. The a in B is longer.

Page 27
2. Function: adjective to verb; meaning: causative, 'make red'.
3. Function: noun to verb; meaning: causative, 'make dangerous'.
4. Function: noun to verb; meaning: 'make into an idol'.
5. Function: verb to adjective; meaning: 'able to be read' or 'good to read'.

Page 33
give:/gɪv/; one syllable, one morpheme; to transfer from one person/object to another; used very widely in a range of metaphorical contexts (give an answer, give up etc).

alligator:/'æligeɪtəɹ/; 4 syllables, one morpheme; a noun; an amphibious reptile; no special contextual features; often shortened to *'gator*.

shit:/ʃɪt/; one syllable, one morpheme; noun or exclamation; excrement, or expression of frustration; often used metaphorically for any unpleasant substance or situation.

peckish:/'pɛkɪʃ/; two syllables, two morphemes; adjective, but not used in front of nouns (*a peckish child) slightly hungry; British, somewhat old-fashioned.

liposuction:/lɪpowsʌkʃəɳ/; four syllables, three morphemes; noun; extraction of fat from body tissue; fashionable surgical procedure for people who wish to look slimmer.

CHAPTER 4

Page 58
1 gradable antonym; 2 hyponym; 3 homophone; 4 hyponym; 5 converse terms; 6 homonym: both homophone and homograph; 7 hyponym; 8 complementary terms; 9 hyponym; 10 synonym.

Page 59
This may not be as easy as it looks at first sight.*Lend* and *borrow, let* and *rent* may be truly complementary, except that in the latter case the word *rent* is nowadays often used for both sides of the transaction. In the case of *teaching* and *learning* it should be noted that teaching does not always lead to learning, and learning can occur without teaching. As for the others, think of sentences like: *I gave her a ring but she refused it. I'm coming to see you. I'm going to see you.* Compare these, if possible, to similar verb pairs in other languages.

Page 61
It should not be necessary for me to provide all the 'solutions'. Your imagination will surely be up to the task. Think of utterances like 'I am somewhat short of funds right now', 'This soup is disgusting!' and so on.

Page 63
Fatally flawed; sincerely yours; undoubtedly true; dazzlingly beautiful; impeccably attired; carefully crafted; solidly built; densely wooded; tastefully furnished; professionally designed; painfully obvious; perfectly plain.

Page 71
1. B; 2. E; 3. F; 4. A; 5. C; 6. D.

Page 76
1. E; 2. A; 3. H; 4. B; 5. G; 6. C; 7. I; 8. D; 9. J; 10. F.

CHAPTER 5

Page 91
Did you eat yet? No, did you? Let's go eat. Okay.

Page 94
Note: I have deliberately left out words that are most often quoted in British/American comparisons, such as lorry/truck, boot/trunk, and so on. If you are a teacher you may want to create your own matching exercises which use better known words.
1. D; 2. H; 3. E; 4. G; 5. I; 6. A (recreational vehicle); 7. B; 8. F; 9. J; 10. C.

CHAPTER 7

Page 118
We whisper in hospitals and become anxious in police stations, sad in cemeteries, docile in schools and jovial at parties.

Page 120
1 Jargon; 2 ethnocentric; 3 xenophobia; 4 gobbledygook; 5 slang; 6 taboo; euphemisms; 7 dialect; 8 anomie.

IPA phonetic symbols

Some rules used in this book:

— Phonemic transcriptions are put between slashes://.
— Phonetic transcriptions (usually showing more detail) are put between square brackets:[].
— Primary and secondary stress are marked as follows: 'tele,phone (see the transcription for *Stachelschwein* on page 17).
— For the English postvocalic /r/ the symbol /ɹ/ is often used (see the transcription of sure and more on page 18).
— In American English the length mark is often not used.

Consonants and vowels

CONSONANTS			VOWELS	
symbol	*keyword*		*symbol*	*keyword*
ɪ	bit		e	bet
æ	bat		ʌ	but
ɒ	pot		ʊ	put
ə	about			
iː	bead		ɑː	bard
ɜː	bird		ɔː	board
uː	food			
eɪ	tail		aɪ	tile
ɔɪ	toil		əʊ	coal
aʊ	cowl		ɪə	pier
eə	pear		ʊə	poor
p	pill		b	big
t	till		d	dig
k	kill		g	gig
f	fin		v	van
θ	thin		ð	than
s	sin		z	zip
ʃ	shin		ʒ	pleasure
h	hill			
m	some			
n	sun			
ŋ	sung			
tʃ	choke		dʒ	joke
l	lay		w	wet
r	ray		j	yet

OTHER SYMBOLS

i	happy, create	u	thank you, throughout
ʔ	(glottal stop)	pʰ, tʰ, kʰ	(aspirated consonant)
ŋ ✶	(syllabic consonant)		
'no	(primary stress) ,notwith 'standing (secondary stress on *not*)		

Further reading

Chapter 1

Andrews, L. 1993. *Language Exploration and Awareness: A Resource Book for Teachers.* London: Longman.
An excellent guide for teachers who wish to explore different ways of making language study relevant for their students (at all levels). Contains many useful activities to stimulate interest and curiosity.

Burrell, K. 1991. *Knowledge About Language.* London: Nelson.
A book of interesting and varied activities intended for secondary school students, but equally relevant as a model for language awareness work at all levels.

Carter, R. (ed.) 1990. *Knowledge About Language and the Curriculum: the LINC reader.* London: Hodder and Stoughton.
A collection of scholarly articles about language education and its place in the National Curriculum.

Chapter 2

Aitchison, J. 1992. *Teach Yourself Linguistics.* Third edition. London: Hodder and Stoughton.
A straightforward introduction to linguistics including an accessible account of Chomsky's theories of transformational grammar and government and binding.

Crystal, D. 1992. *Introducing Linguistics.* London: Penguin.
An alphabetical introduction to the main concepts of linguistics, very useful as a resource and reference guide.

Yule, G. 1985. *The Study of Language.* Cambridge University Press.
A short and well-written introduction to linguistics which effectively introduces all the main topics and includes useful activities using a range of languages.

Chapter 3

Halliday, M. A. K. and R. Hasan. 1989. *Language, Context and Text.* Oxford University Press.
An accessible overview of Halliday and Hasan's model of functional grammar, containing clear accounts of the concepts *field*, *tenor*, and *mode*, analysis of texts and discussion of the main elements of cohesion.

Hatch, E. 1991. *Discourse and Language Education.* Cambridge University Press.
A detailed and thorough textbook on discourse analysis, particularly useful for those working in language teaching, and including a wealth of data, especially spoken, for description and analysis.

Nunan, D. 1994. *Introducing Discourse Analysis.* London: Penguin.
A short introduction to the main concepts in discourse analysis, including a wealth of data from both spoken and written sources as well as a number of activities.

Chapter 4

Aitchison, J. 1987. *Words in the Mind.* Oxford: Basil Blackwell.
An excellent introduction to psycholinguistics, including a thorough discussion on how language is represented in the brain.

Allen, I. L. 1990. *Unkind Words: Ethnic Labelling from Redskin to Wasp.* New York: Bergin and Garvey.
A fascinating discussion of the history and current use of an amazing variety of terms relating to prejudice, racial slurs and ethnic stereotyping.

Gairns, R. and S. Redman 1986. *Working with Words: A Guide to Teaching and Learning Vocabulary.* Cambridge University Press.
A comprehensive and practical discussion of main issues in vocabulary teaching, with a wealth of ideas, techniques and activities for teachers and students.

Chapter 5

Baron, D. E. 1982. *Grammar and Good Taste: Reforming the American Language.* New Haven: Yale University Press.

A detailed and well-written history of language reform in the United States, giving good insights into attitudes towards 'correct' or 'proper' language.

MacAndrew, R. 1991. *English Observed.* Hove: Language Teaching Publications.

A practical guide to make teachers and advanced students reflect on what they mean by 'correct' English and 'making a mistake'. Contains numerous examples and problems to show that the language of the 'real world' is often quite different to that of the textbook or grammar.

Chapter 6

Allwright, D. and K. M. Bailey 1991. *Focus on the Language Classroom.* Cambridge University Press.

A practical discussion of classroom talk and of ways to study it systematically. The book contains many extracts from classroom lessons as well as activities and projects for pre-service and in-service teachers.

Bain, R., B. Fitzgerald, and M. Taylor (eds.) 1992. *Looking Into Language: Classroom Approaches to Knowledge About Language.* London: Hodder and Stoughton.

Contains first-hand accounts of ways in which teachers at different levels have incorporated language awareness work in their own curriculum. The work is systematically related to the guidelines of the British National Curriculum.

van Manen, M. 1989. *The Tact of Teaching.* New York: SUNY Press.

Van Manen focuses on the ways in which teachers interact with students and promotes a reflective attitude towards our words and actions which he calls pedagogical thoughtfulness.

Chapter 7

Bourdieu, P. and L. J. Wacquant, 1992. *An Invitation to Reflexive Sociology.* Chicago University Press.

A reasonably accessible overview of the work of the French sociologist Pierre Bourdieu.

Darder, A. 1991. *Culture and Power in the Classroom.* New York: Bergin and Garvey.

A discussion of critical theory as it applies to educational issues, including multicultural classrooms.

Fairclough, N. 1989. *Language and Power*. London: Longman.
Fairclough's discussion of language and power provides strong arguments for critical discourse analysis and critical language awareness.

Glossary

affix (prefix, infix, suffix) A bound **morpheme** or part of a **word** which is added to a main word and which cannot stand on its own. Prefixes are added at the beginning of a word: *un*-like, *de*-frost; infixes are added in the middle of a word (this is rare – and only used for swearing – in English, though quite common in many languages): inter-*bloody*-national, ha *bloody* ha (if you count *haha* as one word); suffixes are added to the end of a word: use-*less*, tender-*ize*.

allophone two allophones sound different but they do not change meaning, whereas two **phonemes** do. The [t] in *top* and *stop* are allophones of the phoneme /t/: the first is aspirated, the second is not. The [t] in water, as pronounced by most speakers of American English is another allophone of the phoneme /t/. English has only one phoneme /t/, but this phoneme has a number of different allophones. Another way of saying this is that /t/ may sound different depending on what other sounds are around it, or where in the word it occurs.

antonym A word that means the opposite of another word, e.g., *hot* is the antonym of *cold*.

assimilation The influence of one sound on another. For example, the /n/ in unproductive may be pronounced as [m]. Sometimes called absorption patterns, consisting of linking sounds (*the idea-r-is*), levelling (the [m] in *unproductive*), and loss (for example, *fiths* instead of *fifths*) of sounds.

bilingualism The ability to speak two or more languages with some (not necessarily equal) degree of proficiency. Subtractive bilingualism is a situation whereby one language gets replaced by another in a child's education, additive bilingualism refers to learning another language while maintaining the first.

collocation   the habitual occurrence of two or more **words** in each other's vicinity, for example, *loose-leaf binder* (and not loose-*page* binder); a *ten-page memo* (and not a ten-*leaf* memo).

complementary term   See **converse term**

connotation   A meaning of a **word** in addition to its literal or dictionary meaning (denotation), or a feeling suggested by a word. *Cowboy* has a connotation of dishonesty in British English, as in *cowboy builders*.

context   The situation in which a piece of language occurs, including the setting, the participants, the type of activity, and so on. Also, as **linguistic** context (co-text), the other language that surrounds a particular piece of language.

conversation   The most basic form of human **interaction** where the focus is on symmetry between the different contributions. In some accounts conversation is used in a more generic sense of any verbal interaction.

converse term   A word that expresses an opposite but related action to another word e.g., *read* and *write*, *come* and *go*. These terms are closely related to **antonyms**. Some converse terms are complementary, that is, the action expressed in one, is complemented by (and often requires) the action expressed in the other. *Lend* and *borrow, let* and *rent*, are examples, though in the latter case *rent* is often used for both sides of the transaction. An interesting question for those readers who are teachers: are *teach* and *learn* true complementary terms?

critical   An adjective used in critical science, critical theory, critical **discourse analysis**, critical language awareness, critical **linguistics** and so on, to indicate an ideologically based and politically or socially active stance in one's work, rather than a detached and neutral one.

culture   There are numerous definitions of culture. A simple and effective one is 'the way we do things around here.' Some people use culture in the sense of sophisticated products such as art, literature, architecture and so on, and may call this Culture 'with a capital C.' In anthropology and **linguistics**, however, such a distinction between 'big-C' and 'small-c' is not made.

Glossary

dialect A recognizable or recognized variety of a language, associated with particular regions or particular groups of people (for example, Brummie and Scouse in Britain, Appalachian and Brooklynese in the US). From time to time new dialects appear, for example, the British now have 'Estuary English' and the Americans have 'Valley Talk'.

discourse analysis A branch of **pragmatics** (and/or, depending on how you categorize the field, **sociolinguistics**) that analyses units of language larger than the sentence or the **utterance**, in other words, that analyses texts, such as **conversations**, stories, newspaper articles, songs etc.

discourse world A term referring to a particular way of speaking of an identifiable group of people using **words**, expressions and ways of interacting that set them apart and may be difficult for others to follow. Related to **jargon, register**. Computer specialists appear to have their own discourse world, and so do the legal profession, the surfing community, etc.

ESL English as a Second Language. Also variously known as TESOL (Teaching English to Speakers of Other Languages) or ESOL, EFL (English as a Foreign Language – particularly in non-English-medium countries), ELT (English Language Teaching).

function (grammatical, constituency) The role a **word** or group of words plays in a sentence, for example, subject, verb, object (or *actor, action patient* in semantic terms). In a broader, **semantic** sense function means the purpose or use of a word or larger unit. In this sense, the function of a **speech act** like 'Please pass the salt' is to make a <u>request</u>.

grammar In a narrow sense this refers to the structure of sentences, but in a broad sense it includes everything to do with the structure of language. <u>Prescriptive grammar</u> refers to rules and regulations on how one should speak, <u>descriptive grammar</u> refers to an account of how people actually do speak, without making value judgements.

homonym A word that is pronounced and/or written in the same way as another word but has a different meaning. *Bank* (of a river) and *bank* (financial institution) are homonyms; so are *right* and *write*. *See also* **homophone** and **homograph.**

homophone A word that sounds the same as another word, e.g., *bear* is a homophone of *bare*. Some homophones are also homographs; that is, they are written in the same way, *bear* (the animal) and *bear* (to carry) are homophonic and homographic. They are true **homonyms**.

hyponym   A word that is subordinate to another word, e.g., that is a member of a class (*chair* is a hyponym of *furniture, child* is a hyponym of *person*), or whose meaning is included in another word (*stroll* is a hyponym of *walk*, since strolling is a special way of walking).

illocutionary act   *see* **speech act**

illocutionary force   *see* **speech act**

interaction   Two or more actions – verbal or otherwise – that are related to each other.

intonation   The 'melody' of spoken language, where **words** are said on a different pitch, often rising and falling. Intonation generally helps to convey the attitude of the speaker.

jargon   *see* **register**

kinesic, kinesics   Gestures, facial expressions, posture and movements that accompany (and sometimes replace) speech. Also known as body language.

linguistics   The systematic, scientific study of language. Traditionally this was mostly limited to philology, or the history of language, but modern **linguistics** studies a range of aspects of language. Core linguistics tends to be limited to **phonology, morphology** and **syntax,** but **sociolinguistics,** psycholinguistics, **pragmatics**, educational linguistics (among other sub-disciplines) cast their net much more widely.

meta-   A term indicating over or above. Metalinguistic is language about language, or knowledge about language (KAL). Metacognition is thinking about language, or knowledge about thinking.

metaphor   An imaginative and often creative use of **words** to describe something. Many metaphors are part of everyday language, such as the *foot* of a ladder, time *flies*. Metaphors can also be specially created for the occasion, as in 'the stock market went south.'

Glossary

morpheme A **word** or part of a word that has a separate meaning and cannot be divided any further. Words like *table, hat* and *on* are free morphemes, and *pre-, -able, -ly* (as in quick-*ly*, turning an adjective into an verb, and meaning 'in a quick manner') are bound morphemes because they cannot stand on their own. The word *unreadable* can be divided into three morphemes: *un-, read-* and *-able*.

morphology The study of **morphemes** or the form of **words**, including word formation processes such as compounding (making a new word out of two or more words, as in *blackbird, turn-on-and-off-able*).

phoneme The smallest unit of sound that changes the meaning of a word. In English, /t/ and /d/ are separate phonemes, as shown in the minimal pair /tent/ and /dent/. See also **allophone**.

phonetic alphabet A special alphabet used to transcribe exactly how a language sounds. The most commonly used alphabet is the International Phonetic Alphabet (see page 142). Most dictionaries use a phonetic alphabet based on the IPA (Webster's is an exception), but usually with some variations.

phonology The study of the sound system of a particular language, including what distinctive sounds (**phonemes**) there are, and how they can be combined (**phonotactics**).

phonotactics The study of how sounds can be combined in a particular language. For example, in English the combination *bl-* can occur at the beginning of a **word**, but the combination *bn-* cannot. In Spanish the combinations *st-, sp-,* or *sk-* cannot occur at the beginning of words. Phonotactic differences can cause foreign students quite considerable and long-term difficulties.

pragmatics The study of language in **context**, including issues of speakers' intentions and hearers' interpretations.

prosody (suprasegmental features) Deals with issues going beyond the sounds themselves, most notably the <u>rhythm</u> and <u>rate</u> of speech, **stress** patterns, and **intonation**.

register A particular type or variety of language used for a specific purpose (for example, business letters, legal documents, sports broadcasting) or a specialized group of professionals. Closely related to other terms such as genre, variety, **discourse world, jargon** (the latter tends to have a negative connotation of excessive use of specialized language).

schema theory The study of the way information, knowledge and abilities are organized and stored in the brain in terms of networks of related concepts. Also often referred to as background knowledge. Related: frames and scripts, which are more procedural in that they involve a series of steps, such as how to use a restaurant.

semantics The study of meaning, of **words** (lexical semantics: synonymy, antonymy, homonymy etc) or sentences (propositions, truth relations, entailment etc).

sociolinguistics A branch of **linguistics** which studies the relationships between language and social life, including language variation, racial and class issues, gender, interaction and power relationships.

speech act An action carried out in language. For example, firing someone is done by saying 'You're fired!' Of course, for such a **speech act** to 'count', certain conditions must be met. In the case of firing, a relationship of boss–worker must obtain, and so on. A special case of speech acts, called **illocutionary acts**, refer to the speaker's intentions in uttering something. For example, the **illocutionary force** of 'Look out!' is a warning.

stress The prominence of certain **syllables** in a **word**, or words in a sentence. This may be achieved by loudness (more vocal power), lengthening of a vowel, raising of pitch, or in other ways. Many languages have characteristic stress patterns, (for example, English tends to place stress at regular intervals, it is stress-timed whereas other languages may be syllable-timed, that is, each syllable achieves a basic amount of stress, i.e. Finnish, in which it is always the first syllable that is stressed the most). Sometimes the word accent is used to denote stress, but in that context it must not be confused with its more everyday use, for example, in regional accent, or foreign accent.

syllable A unit which is quite hard to define, but which is of fundamental importance in the production and interpetation of speech. Every syllable basically has its own peak of prominence, though some will stand out more than others. It is sometimes jokingly defined as 'what the word *syllable* has three of'.

synonym A word that has the same meaning as another word: *car* and *automobile* are synonyms. Note that in most (if not all) cases, synonyms cannot automatically replace each other in all contexts. For example, a daughter is unlikely to ask her father: 'Can I borrow your automobile' (the word car is more likely here).

syntax The part of **grammar** which studies the way **words** are combined into sentences, how they are grouped into constituents and phrases (for example, *the pale student* sighed; *what I mean is* that you can't . . .) and the rules of word order and systematic changes in word order.

turn taking The procedures that govern changes in speakership in spoken **interaction**, so that overlaps and silences are minimized, and orderly transitions are assured. Turn taking was first addressed in depth by ethnomethodology, a branch of sociology interested in the study of every-day practices, especially **conversation**.

utterance The equivalent of sentence in spoken **interaction**; a contribution by one speaker, before and after which there is silence on the part of that speaker.

word The basic building block of language, consisting of one or more **morphemes**, and treated as one conceptual unit.

References

Allwright, D. and K. M. Bailey 1991. *Focus on the Language Classroom.* Cambridge: Cambridge University Press.

Aitchison, J. 1992. *Teach Yourself Linguistics.* Third edition. London: Hodder and Stoughton.

Atkinson, J. M. 1984. *Our Masters' Voices.* London: Methuen.

Bain, R., B. Fitzgerald and M. Taylor (eds.) 1992. *Looking into Language: Classroom Approaches to Knowledge About Language.* London: Hodder and Stoughton.

Bakhtin, M. M. 1981. *The Dialogic Imagination.* Austin: The University of Texas Press.

Baron, D. 1982. *Grammar and Good Taste.* New Haven: Yale University Press.

Benson, M., E. Benson and R. Ilson. 1986. *The BBI Combinatory Dictionary of English: A Guide to Word Combination.* Amsterdam: John Benjamins.

Berger, P. and T. Luckmann. 1966. *The Social Construction of Reality.* London: Penguin.

Bolinger, D. 1980. *Language, the Loaded Weapon: the Use and Abuse of Language Today.* London: Longman.

Bolinger, D. and D. Sears. 1981. *Aspects of Language.* New York: Harcourt, Brace, Jovanovich.

Bourdieu, P. 1990. *The Logic of Practice.* Palo Alto, CA: Stanford University Press.

Bourdieu, P. 1991. *Language and Symbolic Power.* Cambridge, MA: Harvard University Press.

Carter, R. (ed.) 1990. *Knowledge About Language and the Curriculum: the LINC Reader.* London: Hodder and Stoughton.

Carter, R. 1992. *Language in the National Curriculum: Lecture Notes.* London: Thames Valley University.

References

Chomsky, N. 1965. *Aspects of a Theory of Syntax.* Cambridge, MA: The MIT Press.

Davidson, D. 1984. *What Metaphors Mean.* (From D. Davidson. *Inquiries into Truth and Interpretation.* Oxford: Oxford University Press.)

DES. 1975. *A Language for Life: The Bullock Report.* London: Her Majesty's Stationery Office.

DES 1988. *The Kingman Report.* London: Her Majesty's Stationery Office.

Donmall, G. (ed.) 1985. *Language Awareness.* London: CILT.

Ervin-Tripp, S. M. 1972. *Sociolinguistic Rules of Address.* (From J. B. Pride and J. Holmes (eds.) *Sociolinguistics.* London: Penguin.)

Fairclough, N. 1989. *Language and Power.* London: Longman.

Flesch, R. 1951. *The Art of Clear Thinking.* New York: Barnes and Noble.

Freire, P. 1972. *The Pedagogy of the Oppressed.* New York: Herder and Herder.

Gardner, H. 1989. *To Open Minds.* New York: Basic Books.

Gardner, H. 1991. *The Unschooled Mind.* New York: Basic Books.

Goffman, E. 1981. *Forms of Talk.* Oxford: Basil Blackwell.

Goodman, Y. 1989. *Language Invention and Social Convention.* Plenary Session, 23rd Annual TESOL Convention, San Antonio, Texas, March 1989.

Gramsci, A. 1985. *Selections from Cultural Writings.* (From D. Forgacs and N. Smith (eds.) London: Lawrence & Wishart.)

Greene, J. 1985. *Understanding Language: A Cognitive Approach.* Milton Keynes: Open University Press.

Grice, P. 1989. *Logic and Conversation* (From P. Grice, *Studies in the Way of Words.* Cambridge, MA: Harvard University Press.)

Gumperz, J. 1982. *Discourse Strategies.* Cambridge: Cambridge University Press.

Habermas, J. 1984. *The Theory of Communicative Action,* Volume 1. Boston: Beacon Press.

Halliday, M. A. K. 1982. *Linguistics in Teacher Education.* (From R. Carter (ed.) *Linguistics and the Teacher.* London: Routledge and Kegan Paul.)

Halliday, M. A. K. 1989. *Spoken and Written Language.* Oxford: Oxford University Press.

Hatch, E. 1992. *Discourse and Language Education*. Cambridge: Cambridge University Press.

James, C. and P. Garrett (eds.) 1991. *Language Awareness in the Classroom*. London: Longman.

Joos, M. 1967. *The Five Clocks*. New York: Harcourt, Brace, Jovanovich.

Langer, E. 1989. *Mindfulness*. Reading, MA: Addison-Wesley.

Leech, G. 1983. *Principles of Pragmatics*. London: Longman.

Lewis, C. S. 1960. *Studies in Words*. Cambridge: Cambridge University Press.

Longman, 1993. *Longman Language Activater*. London: Longman.

Mitchell, R. and J. Hooper 1991. *Teachers' Views of Language Knowledge*. (From C. James and P. Garrett (eds.) *Language Awareness in the Classroom*. London: Longman.)

Nunan, D. 1993. *Introducing Discourse Analysis*. London: Penguin.

Polanyi, M. 1958. *Personal Knowledge*. London: Routledge and Kegan Paul.

Prabhu, N. S. 1987. *Second Language Pedagogy*. Oxford: Oxford University Press.

Rabinow, P. 1984. *A Foucault Reader*. New York: Pantheon Books.

Ravetz, J. 1971. *Scientific Knowledge and its Social Problems*. Oxford: Oxford University Press.

Sapir 1921. *Language*. New York: Harcourt, Brace and World, Inc.

Scheglogg, E. A. 1984. *On Some Questions and Ambiguities in Conversation*. (From J. M. Atkinson and J. Heritage (eds.) *Structures of Social Action*. Cambridge: Cambridge University Press.)

Sinclair, J. McH. and M. Coulthard 1975. *Towards an Analysis of Discourse*. Oxford: Oxford University Press.

Spolsky, B. 1978. *Educational Linguistics*. Rowley, MA: Newbury House.

Stenhouse, L. 1975. *Introduction to Curriculum Research and Development*. London: Heinemann.

Stubbs, M. 1986. *Educational Linguistics*. Oxford: Basil Blackwell.

Tannen, D. 1987. *That's Not What I Meant*. London: Dent.

Tannen, D. 1990. *You Just Don't Understand*. New York: Morrow.

van Lier, L. 1989. *Reeling, Writhing, Drawling, Stretching and Fainting in Coils: Oral Proficiency Interviews as Conversation*. TESOL Quarterly. 23, 3, 489–508.

van Lier, L. 1994. *Educational Linguistics: Field and Project*. Washington,

References

DC: Georgetown University Round Table for Languages and Linguistics.

Vygotsky, L. S. 1962. *Thought and Language*. Cambridge, MA: The MIT Press.

Wajnrayb, R. 1993. *Classroom Observation Tasks*. Cambridge: Cambridge University Press.

Wertsch, J. 1991. *Voices of the Mind*. Hemel Hempstead: Simon and Schuster.

Yule, G. 1985. *The Study of Language*. Cambridge: Cambridge University Press.

Index

Index

Corson, D., 117
critical language awareness, 37,
    117–136
cross-cultural, 6, 127
culture, cultural 6, 11, 47, 52, 55,
    64, 68, 120, 122
— multiculturalism, 117, 122, 135
— ritual, 62, 68
curriculum, 100–104, 108, 115

Davidson, D., 65
derivation, 26, 27
dialect, 7, 19, 81, 92–97, 120–122,
    130, 136
dialogic, 48
dictionary, 77, 135
discourse, 44, 69, 119
dysphemism, 60, 76

education, 7–10, 95, 97, 98–116
error, 73, 78
ethnocentric, 120
euphemism, 60, 76, 120

Fairclough, N., 117
false cognate, 41
Fitzgerald, B., 108
Flesch, 99
focal awareness, 3, 4, 10
focus on language, 4
footing, 51
foreign language teaching/learning,
    7, 8, 36, 99, 111, 131
Foucault, M., 117
frame, 49, 54
Freire, P., 117
function, 13, 30

Gardner, H., 65
gender, 135

genre, 66
gobbledygook, 76, 120
Goffman, E., 51
Goodman, Y., 66
Green, J., 62
Grice, P., 49
grammar 7, 8, 105
— formal, 106, 131
— prescriptive, 8
— tolerance, 82, 85
— traditional, 47
grapheme, 16
Gumperz, 23

Habermas, J., 117
Halliday, 87, 88, 108
Hatch, E., 55
Hoffman, 131
homonym, 58
homophone, 58
Hooper, J., 108
hyponym, 58, 59

idiom, 66–69, 73
infix, 28
intention, 41, 46, 78
interaction, 48, 109–116
International Phonetic Alphabet
    (IPA), 17, 141
interpretation, interpretive, 41, 46,
    47, 51, 54, 78, 136
intonation, 22–24, 42–43, 55, 62, 88
IRF exchange, 110, 116

jargon, 120
Johnson, Samuel, 28
Joos, M., 83

KAL, 9
kinesic(s), 43–44, 55, 88

159

Index